PRACTICAL LANGUAGE TEACHING

Editors: Marion Geddes and Gill Sturtridge

No. 7

Video in the Language Classroom

D0332608

PRACTICAL LANGUAGE TEACHING
Editors: Marion Geddes and Gill Sturtridge

Acknowledgements

Acknowledgement is due to the following for permission to reproduce photographs used in the text:

The British Council
Colorado State University
University of Lancaster
Elayne Phillips
Sony (UK) Limited
Video Arts Limited
Claire Woolford

Video in the Language Classroom

Edited by MARION GEDDES
and GILL STURTRIDGE

HEINEMANN EDUCATIONAL BOOKS
London

Heinemann Educational Books Ltd.
22 Bedford Square, London WC1B 3HH

LONDON   EDINBURGH   MELBOURNE   AUCKLAND
HONG KONG   SINGAPORE   KUALA LUMPUR
NEW DELHI   IBADAN   NAIROBI   JOHANNESBURG
EXETER (NH)   KINGSTON   PORT OF SPAIN

British Library Cataloguing in Publication Data

Video in the language classroom. – (Practical
  language teaching; no.7)
  1. Language and languages – Study and teaching –
  Audio-visual aids
  I. Geddes, Marion
  II. Sturtridge, Gill   III. Series
  371.3'3   P53

ISBN 0 435 28971 3

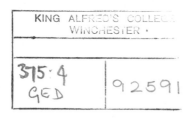
Set in 10 on 12 point Times by Typesetters (Birmingham) Ltd,
and printed in Great Britain
by Hazell Watson & Viney Ltd, Aylesbury, Bucks

Contents

Introduction

When video recorders first became readily available in the 1970s they seemed to offer exciting new possibilities for language teaching and learning. Many institutions invested considerable sums of money in buying such equipment as a videotape recorder and a monitor or television receiver; sometimes a small video camera; and sometimes even a closed-circuit TV studio complex. It seemed obvious to all of us that learning materials that added a moving visual element to sound could make language more alive and meaningful and could help bring the real world into the classroom. Alas, a decade later much of this equipment sits collecting dust. It is perhaps used occasionally but more often it is referred to as the school's white elephant.

Slowly we are learning how to make better use of the products of engineering and technology, but our efforts are often still tentative and experimental in nature, accompanied by failures as well as successes. However, for progress to be made, both failures and successes must be shared and ideas exchanged and developed. This is the purpose of our book. We do not believe that the state of the art is sufficiently developed for one person to sit down and write a book on the use of video in language learning. We have preferred to invite practising teachers, working in a variety of situations and countries, to say what contribution they feel video can make to language learning and to describe ways in which they have used video with their students. We hope that their experience and ideas will encourage others, provoke discussion, and spark off new ideas.

The scope of this book has been deliberately limited. Its principal concern is the role of video in the presentation and practice of language. Broader discussions of the use of video for other aspects of language learning, for example for language assessment, have been excluded. Also excluded is any consideration of the role of video in teacher training. This seems to us to be such an important area that it demands a volume in its own right to do it justice. We hope that by thus restricting our focus we have managed to make it sharper.

How any teaching aid is used obviously depends on how the user understands the nature of language learning. With video, however, users tend to get entangled in the complexities of the technology before they are able to consider how to use it. Certainly the question of how to use video is closely related to the nature of the equipment available. In the early rush of enthusiasm, some people assumed that if one had everything and invested in a full-scale studio set-up it would be possible to achieve much more than if one had a single camera or perhaps only a videotape recorder capable of recording programmes off air from a domestic television receiver. The irony of this apparent logic is that, generally speaking, the greatest use of video has probably occurred in schools and institutions where large-scale facilities do not exist. Here teachers have escaped becoming entangled in the technology and have not felt intimidated by lack of technical training. Instead they have worked with teaching colleagues without technical help. Using less sophisticated equipment they could either make recordings with a single camera or try to find ways of exploiting ready-made material that was either recorded off air from a television receiver, purchased or borrowed.

In chapter 1, Margaret Allan discusses the options available and the kind of decisions involved when choosing and adding to video equipment. If more people had been aware of these options in the early days of video there might be fewer disillusioned people today. Unfortunately, one major technical problem has changed little in the last decade: the lack of standardisation between equipment from different manufacturers, and the changing specifications that can make last year's model incompatible with this year's.

A two-camera system with the necessary switching equipment might be intimidating for some and require more people to use it; but there is no teacher who cannot learn how to use simple portable recording equipment with one camera. Claire Woolford in chapter 2 gives practical advice on how to gain confidence and expertise in handling such equipment and so get the most out of it. Those who find their two or three camera set-ups difficult to use, for whatever reason, might consider cutting their losses and try using only part of the equipment, making recordings with one camera. At a later date they can take the experience gained with one camera back to the more sophisticated set-up. Instead of seeing this equipment as a series of technical hurdles, their increased confidence should allow them to appreciate what the additional technical facilities can help them achieve.

The single camera can be used in a variety of ways. It can be used to record teaching material. Marion Geddes in chapter 3 shows how the simplest of all recordings, the 'talking head', can be used profitably in study skills classes and in chapter 4 Eddie Williams describes how silent sequences, shot with one camera, can be used to encourage group oral interaction. Stephen Hick, Gareth Hughes and Christopher Stott in chapter 5 describe how they have used a single camera to monitor students' performances. Because the single camera is easy to operate it can also be handed over to students to operate themselves. Elayne Phillips in chapter 6 and Gill Sturtridge in chapter 7 describe learning activities where students, instead of being simply receivers of video, have discovered how to produce it.

All users and would-be users of video are aware of the immensely rich supply of raw material available from off-air recordings and commercially produced films and videotapes. A major problem lies of course in the fact that their producers never intended their work to be used for language teaching. How can the language teacher exploit this apparent potential? Three contributors, David Kerridge (chapter 8), Susan Sheerin (chapter 9) and Valerie Bevan (chapter 10), describe how they have used some of this material with students studying English for specific purposes (ESP) – business, medicine and civil engineering. Their ideas for exploiting video material can be equally well applied to other specific areas and to general English.

When using other people's film and video materials, questions of copyright cannot be ignored. In chapter 11 Geoffrey Crabb gives a helpful guide through this maze.

For practical reasons of time, money and training, closed-circuit studio facilities in language teaching institutions are likely to remain under-utilised for a long time to come. This is not to say that they should therefore be ignored, particularly if the material produced in them is designed not only for the institution that owns the studio but can be made available to others. Mary Ann Telatnik and William Kruse in chapter 12 describe the cultural videotapes they were able to make using the studio facilities of Colorado State University. The time and money spent on these productions have resulted in visually attractive material of a high technical quality, and the content and aims of these tapes are suited to ESL programmes at other North American universities.

The time spent by the British Council in Iran in producing the Basic Oral Communication Skills in English (BOCS) video materials, described by Gill Jones in chapter 13, also makes economic sense when one realises that these materials were designed and produced not for one institute but for five sister institutes as well.

Unfortunately the size of our book limits the number of teachers we have been able to invite to contribute. We know of other teachers who are doing equally interesting work. And we know that there must be many more whose work we have not yet been fortunate enough to see. (We hope that this book may encourage them to write to us and tell us how they have been using video.) We have also had to exclude discussion of the use of video material commercially produced for language teaching, such as is available from BBC English by Television. Fortunately the BBC and some teachers are sharing their experience through conferences and journals.

If you are thinking of buying video equipment we hope this book will help you make decisions about what to buy and how to use it. If you already have video equipment which is not often used, we hope this book will help change your white elephant into a much valued and useful pet.

Marion Geddes
Gill Sturtridge

1   A Guide to Hardware Options

MARGARET ALLAN

After teaching English as a foreign language for several years, Margaret Allan trained in educational television production and worked in Iran for four years as British Council Educational Technology Officer. She now works in the Council's Media Production Unit in London.

1   INTRODUCTION

What do ELT institutions do with video equipment?

Some use it in teacher training, to take trainees into other people's classrooms or to let them see themselves as others see them.

Others see it as the best medium for bringing reality into the classroom − and it's so much easier to use than a film projector.

In some places students make their own programmes.

In others it hardly ever sees the light of day.

Video can have a range of functions in a language teaching institute and the choice of equipment − hardware − will depend on what the institute wants to use it for. It's important to know what the possibilities are, otherwise it's only too easy to end up with an expensive white elephant.

For detailed technical advice you must go to a video engineer, but you can only make the most of technical expertise if you are clear about what the machines can do and what you want them to do for you. This chapter will outline the basic choices and will relate these, where relevant, to possible uses in an English language teaching or teacher training programme. The hardware options are described under two broad headings:

Playback − the equipment needed in order to replay programmes recorded on video. This section also looks at what is needed to make copies of video recordings and of television programmes (off-air recording).
Own recording − the choices to be made when you want to make your own video recordings.

2 PLAYBACK: USES

What materials are there? Is the software suitable? This is the main consideration if you are going to have playback only. You are dependent on materials produced by other people. The first thing to be done, therefore, is to research what there is, to find out if there is anything that will meet your needs.

(a) *Video inputs to the teaching syllabus*
Types of material and different uses are discussed elsewhere in this book, but you should be clear that the choice is limited. Most published video materials available at the moment were originally designed for broadcast or widescale distribution on film. This applies to many of the BBC English by radio and TV series and to the whole range of non-ELT documentaries which may be applicable to certain language learning needs − particularly in

ESP. The 'designed for broadcast' description of course also applies to material copied off air — the main source of material for institutions in the UK (see chapter 11 on copyright).

Compare this range of material (programmes lasting 20 to 25 minutes, which are self-contained units) with most other resources available to the language teacher in the classroom. The non-video resources have usually been designed for language teaching use under the control of the teacher, and they will very often have been designed as an integral part of a syllabus.

A decision to install video playback should, therefore, take into account not only the software available and its limitations but also the need to help teachers with ideas about how to use it, as well as the need to train them in operating the equipment.

(b)   *Video inputs to teacher training programmes*

Again, the question is, Does the existing software meet our needs? The material available falls into two main categories:

1   *Presents a model* — specially planned to show good examples of a method or a technique. These are usually film series, such as *View and Teach, Teaching Observed*, and the British Council's English Language Teaching Institute films. They are also of course available on video.
2   *Source material* — recordings such as those available from the Inner London Education Authority's Learning Materials Service; or raw recordings, not specially planned as models, that provide data on classroom interaction, teaching styles, etc. which can be the focus for a range of tasks for the trainee teacher.

It is the second type of material that institutions may well consider producing for themselves and this is discussed in section 5 on doing one's own recording.

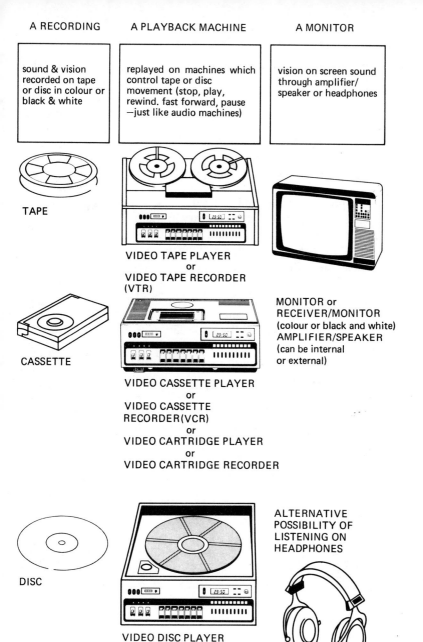

A RECORDING	A PLAYBACK MACHINE	A MONITOR
sound & vision recorded on tape or disc in colour or black & white	replayed on machines which control tape or disc movement (stop, play, rewind, fast forward, pause —just like audio machines)	vision on screen sound through amplifier/ speaker or headphones

TAPE

VIDEO TAPE PLAYER
or
VIDEO TAPE RECORDER
(VTR)

CASSETTE

VIDEO CASSETTE PLAYER
or
VIDEO CASSETTE
RECORDER(VCR)
or
VIDEO CARTRIDGE PLAYER
or
VIDEO CARTRIDGE RECORDER

MONITOR or
RECEIVER/MONITOR
(colour or black and white)
AMPLIFIER/SPEAKER
(can be internal
or external)

DISC

VIDEO DISC PLAYER

ALTERNATIVE
POSSIBILITY OF
LISTENING ON
HEADPHONES

Figure 1

3 PLAYBACK: OPTIONS

To replay video you need:

As Figure 1 shows, there are several choices to be made.

TAPE, CASSETTE, CARTRIDGE OR DISC

Open spool, cassette and cartridge are different formats for housing video tape. The tape can vary in width — ¼″, ½″, ¾″, 1″ and 2″ (metric 6.25mm, 12.5mm, 18mm, 25mm, 50mm). The wider the tape, the better the quality and the more expensive the tape and the machines. Professional broadcasting uses 2″ and 1″; most common for institutional use is ¾″ and ½″. Of the three tape formats, cartridge has never established itself widely.

Discs are not yet established, but could in the future be strong contenders for educational use because of the more accurate control they allow: unlike tape players, disc players give rapid and precise access to any point in the recording. This gives possibilities of video disc/computer combinations which are of considerable interest for self-access language problems, e.g. the video disc plays back a scene, and the learner carries out a range of related tasks via the computer. A disadvantage of disc for some is that you cannot make your own recordings, whereas with the other three formats you can record and re-record, erasing the previous programme in the same way as you can with audio tape.

OPEN SPOOL OR CASSETTE?

This is the most common choice at the time of writing. For institutional use cassette is the most convenient, as it is easier to load and better protected from dust and manhandling. Cassette formats vary in the shape of the container and the width of the tape. The ¾″ — called U-matic — is a popular format for institutions, as the playback machines have proved sturdier than the ½″ machines commonly used in the home.

PLAYER OR RECORDER?

With open spool and cassette machines there is a choice between a player – a machine which plays back only – and a recorder, which is needed if you want to copy from another machine or, with a suitably adapted machine, to copy off air.

Players are cheaper, and institutions which install more than one video machine often have a combination of the two – perhaps two recorders (allowing one spare for breakdowns) and the rest players. Both will play back either colour or black and white.

COMPATIBILITY

(a) *Within the UK*
It is obvious from this range of choices that, for example, the speaker who arrives to give a talk illustrated by a video cassette could easily find that the assurance 'Yes, we have a video machine' turns out to mean that there is a ½" open spool machine waiting for him – no use at all of course. You cannot take anything for granted with equipment – especially not with video equipment. U-matic (¾") cassettes will not play back on ½" cassette machines. One make of ½" cassette machine will not accept ½" cassettes recorded on another. Makes in the same group are compatible with each other, but are incompatible with all makes in other groups (see Table 1).

So it is obviously important to specify your format in advance and in detail if you want to use a tape or machine belonging to someone else. Given time and the right combination of equipment it is of course possible to copy, say, a recording that is on ½" open spool on to a U-matic cassette and vice versa.

(b) *International variations*
If you want to play recordings back in one country that have been made in another, there are further complications. Four different colour codings have been developed in different parts of the world. Even with monochrome recordings, differences in line and field frequencies together with mains frequency variations lead to international incompatibility (see Table 2).

Table 1

Format	Make
1″ open reel	Ampex range
1″ open reel	Shibaden, Sony
¾″ high band U-matic cassette	Sony
¾″ U-matic cassette	Hitachi, JVC, National Panasonic, Sony
½″ open reel EIAJ standard (high energy)	National Panasonic, Sanyo, Shibaden
½″ open reel (high energy)	Sony AV series
½″ cartridge (high energy)	Hitachi, National Panasonic
½″ open reel (low energy)	Sony CV series
½″ cassette	Akai, Grundig, Philips 1500, Philips 1502, Philips 1700, Philips 2020
½″ VHS cassette	Akai, JVC, Hitachi, National Panasonic
½″ Betamax cassette	Sanyo, Sony, Toshiba
¼″ open reel	Akai

Note: this list aims to cover the main makes, but it is not comprehensive.

Table 2

Colour coding	Main users*	Line frequency	Field frequency
PAL	Germany, UK	625	50
SECAM	France, some Middle East countries, USSR	625	50
NTSC	Japan, some Latin American countries, USA	525	60
PAL-M	Argentina, Brazil	525	60

*There are charts which give full details for all countries.

With the U-matic and VHS formats there are multi-standard machines that will switch from PAL to SECAM to NTSC. Otherwise it is also possible to have recordings converted from one standard to another, but this is a special service and normally very expensive.

SECOND TRACK RECORDING

Some video recorders will record and play back two separate sound tracks. If, for instance, the original sound is recorded on track one, an alternative sound track can be recorded on track two. This has obvious applications in language teaching, both for the provision of simplified commentaries and for the recording by students of their own audio versions.

MONITORS

(a) *Monitor, TV receiver/monitor and domestic TV set. What's the difference?*
A *monitor* receives audio and video signals from a video player or recorder. It is not equipped to receive broadcast television signals.

A *domestic TV set* receives broadcast television signals but it is not built to accept the audio and video signals from a video player/ recorder. You can link a domestic TV set to a video player/ recorder by means of a radio frequency (RF) modulator − this allows playback but not off-air recording. One videocassette recorder format − VHS − will record and play back TV signals.

A *TV receiver/monitor* performs the dual function of a monitor and a domestic TV set. Linked to a video recorder, it will receive and record broadcast TV signals and it will also play back video and audio signals from the video recorder. It is common nowadays for video recorders to have a built-in timer, which can be pre-set to switch on to record a particular TV programme.

(b) *Internal or external amplifier/speaker?*
Sound quality is improved by using speakers larger than those normally built in to a monitor or TV receiver. In large classrooms

an external amplifier/speaker is definitely to be recommended. The cost of this can be offset by getting a monitor without an internal speaker.

(c)   *Size and position of screen*

For a classroom seating 20 to 30, a big screen is necessary – 24″, or at least 18″. The monitor should also be raised up for good sightlines (there are special trolleys for this) and they are best placed against the light to avoid reflection on the screen. For larger rooms and numbers, e.g. a lecture hall, it is possible to buy a video projector which projects an image from a normal size monitor on to a film screen, enlarging it to fit that area. The alternative is to have several monitors fitted at different positions in the hall.

COLOUR OR BLACK AND WHITE?

There have been experiments to find out whether colour helps learning more than black and white, but none so far have proved conclusive. Most programmes are made in colour these days and if you play them back in black and white you may lose detail: some colours appear as the same shade of grey on a black and white monitor. And there is of course the subjective impression – colour looks better. Most VTRs and VCRs will play back both colour and black and white. What decides whether you see colour or not is:

(a) The original material.
(b) The monitor you have. Some play back black and white only, and currently cost considerably less than those that also play back colour. However, as the technology develops the price gap is likely to narrow.

STOP FRAME

The *pause* mode on some machines gives you a still picture on the screen, known as a *stop frame* or *freeze frame*. Not all machines have this facility – some simply give a blank screen when paused – and it could well be worth specifying for a machine to be used in language teaching.

4 DISTRIBUTION SYSTEMS

Distribution to classrooms can be done in one of two basic ways:

(1) A closed-circuit system distributes a video signal from one central source to a range of monitors. The signal may come from a video player or recorder or it may come direct from the cameras in a closed-circuit TV studio.

A CCTV system can operate within one building, or a compound can be wired so that rooms in several buildings can receive the signal. It is also possible for a CCTV system to serve all the schools in a city: the education authorities of Inner London and Glasgow were two well-known examples of this.

With an institutional system a teacher asks to have a particular programme played into a particular room at a particular time. A technician (or a computer) then operates the machine. This means that playback machines can be used more economically but there is an obvious loss of flexibility for the teacher. It is important that there should be some form of remote control particularly with a language class, so that the teacher can stop, rewind and replay at will.

(2) The alternative − and nowadays more popular − method is to have complete playback systems in as many rooms as required, or to have a number of mobile systems on trolleys. In this case teachers need to be trained to operate the equipment (not difficult) and a system for distributing and retrieving the recorded cassettes or tapes has to be worked out.

5 OWN RECORDING: USES

The kind of equipment normally installed to meet the recording needs of one institution is known as *small format*. This is non-broadcast standard, and is designed for do-it-yourself domestic use. The results are usually of do-it-yourself domestic standards too. They may meet internal needs perfectly well but, unless backed up by engineering and production know-how and a considerable amount of extra equipment, they are best kept within the institution that produced them.

Given those reservations, however, a recording facility can have a useful function in teacher training programmes and direct teaching.

IN TEACHER TRAINING PROGRAMMES

Teacher training is the reason most frequently given by institutions for acquiring video. This is not surprising, because video's capacity to record the complex activity of a classroom and thereafter replay this record for analysis and discussion makes it a very useful tool. The most common use of video recording in teacher training is in microteaching, but it should be stressed that video is not essential to a microteaching programme − there are several other ways of making a record of what goes on in a class.

Apart from microteaching, an institute might use its video camera(s) to build up a bank of classroom recordings or to record models of various kinds. These types of material have already been mentioned. The main points to make on the production side are:

1   *Source Material*
Source material is only really useful − and therefore likely to be used − if someone has the job of viewing and logging (or discarding) every classroom recording. A simple dub editing facility of the kind described on page 33 would also economise on time if there are identifiable categories of classroom activity, behaviour, etc, that could be assembled on one tape.

2   *Model lessons*
These productions will obviously be planned in advance − the more planning the better, so that before any recording is done, you know exactly what the final order of events will be in the finished programme. This kind of production is probably intended for wider circulation than the others described and, to achieve

acceptable standards, really needs technical and production expertise as well as more sophisticated editing facilities.

IN TEACHING PROGRAMMES

There are two distinct uses of the camera in a teaching programme:

1 *To record student activities*
These are role-plays or simulations which students work up for recording of final performance. Small format video is simple to operate and students can do the recording themselves (see chapters 6 and 7). Recordings of students can also be used for analytical work of various kinds (see chapter 5).

2 *To record teaching material*
This kind of production is in a similar category to the model lessons production and the same reservations apply. It is very easy for enthusiastic teachers to get carried away with plans to produce all kinds of realistic materials and playlets. The do-it-yourself nature of small format video encourages such ideas, which may be excellent but, without professional back-up, the final product is likely to be disappointingly amateurish. This may not matter. Students are often amused and indeed feel involved to see materials produced within their own institute by their own teachers. Students in other institutes, however, might not identify quite so closely, which means that home-made material of this kind will have very limited circulation.

It is of course possible to aim for very simple recording, when the camera is used to allow students to observe a situation. This is often a useful function for ESP work where an unedited, fairly static recording of, for example, a business negotiation would be a valuable resource for language analysis and comprehension work.

6   OWN RECORDING: OPTIONS

To record video material you need:

Figure 2   *Camera plus viewfinder and lens, and video recorder*

You will probably want:

Figure 3 *Monitor, operator, camera tripod, microphone, stand*

Figure 3 — *continued*

But of course it isn't as simple as that. There are also a series of choices to be made.

PORTABLE OR NON-PORTABLE?

The basic difference here is in the video recorder. With a portable system you have a small, light, portable VTR or VCR. It can run off a battery housed within it, so if you keep to the absolute basics there are few cables and it is quick and easy to set up.
A portable kit usually contains:

— camera + viewfinder + zoom lens + internal microphone
— external microphone + table stand
— small portable VTR or VCR, operated off battery or mains
— tripod
— mains adaptor
— battery pack (check life of charged battery — some only last 20′)
— In addition, a colour system has a colour control unit
— A portable monitor can be added

Figure 4 *Portable monitor, colour control unit, colour portable camera*

Figure 4 – *continued*

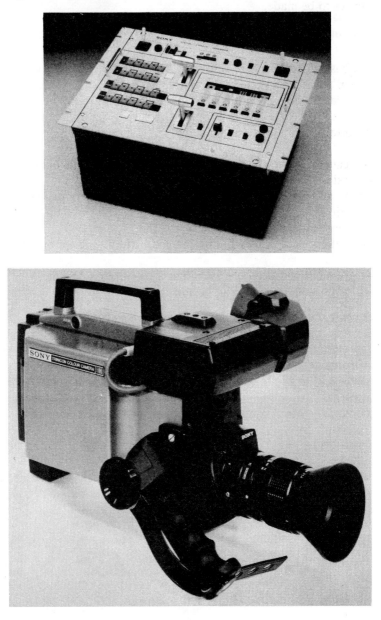

Black and white technology has now reached the point where you can get a perfectly acceptable clear picture in normal indoor lighting. Some colour cameras definitely need additional artificial light and there are portable lights, known as *redheads*, which are usually used with portable colour systems.

Uses of a portable system
It is a good idea to start the own recording venture with a portable system. With it you can do the following:

— take the camera into different classrooms
— record in a range of locations
— run off a battery, if there is no mains available
— link the portable VTR or VCR to a second machine for copying
— link the portable VTR or VCR to a classroom monitor for immediate playback of a recording.

So you start small and flexible and have an opportunity to test out your ideas on uses of a recording facility.

A non-portable system
If you already have a video recorder and want a cheaper small start, you can have a non-portable system by adding a camera and a microphone to the video recorder. The normal size VTR or VCR one would install in a classroom for regular use is bigger and heavier than a portable machine and should not be moved around too much. This is not a problem if you are going to do most of your recording in one room; for example, if you created a video classroom to which classes come for recording. It is possible to get a camera that is compatible with a portable and a non-portable recorder, so that you can start with one and add the other later.

SINGLE CAMERA OR MULTIPLE CAMERA: OR DO YOU NEED A STUDIO?

In the small format context, a studio may simply be a video classroom − a room where the recording equipment is permanently set up so that classes are brought to the camera rather than the reverse. On the other hand, it could be a specially designed CCTV studio, properly soundproofed and with a fully equipped control room — and of course the trained staff to operate and maintain it.

In a teaching institution, the main reason given for getting video recording is often teacher training. It is also often assumed that to record teacher and students in a classroom it is necessary to install a two-camera studio. The point needs to be made that this is not essential. An adequate recording of both teacher and student activities can be achieved with a set-up as shown in Figure 5.

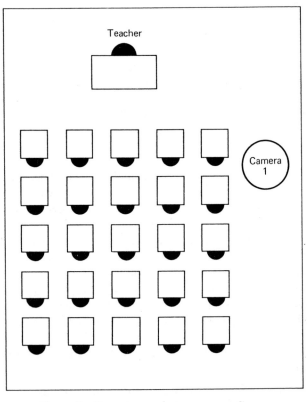

Figure 5   *One-camera classroom recording*

Two cameras would be set up something like this:

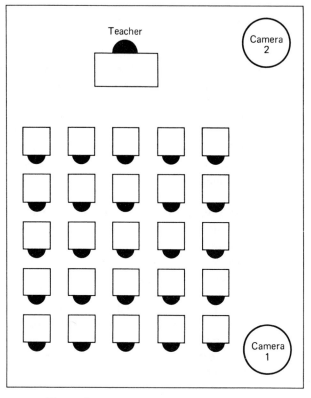

Figure 6   *Two-camera classroom recording*

The addition of a second camera means that one camera can follow the teacher while the other concentrates on the class, giving a choice of pictures.

It would be possible to make two separate recordings with each camera linked to its own video recorder. This allows for later analysis of both recordings, before sequences are selected and edited together to build up an impression of the lesson which focuses on the aspects most relevant to particular training needs.

This, however, is a time-consuming process and requires editing skills.

The more usual way to record with more than one camera is to have the camera signals fed through a vision mixer. The operator views on small monitors the picture each camera is offering. Only one camera signal at a time is recorded, with the operator cutting from one to the other as seems appropriate at the time. This kind of system needs a separate control area – often an adjacent room – to house the equipment.

If the vision mixer has a special effects bank it is possible to record *split screen*, so that the viewer can see both teacher and class on the screen at the same time.

It is also possible to have remote control cameras operated from the control room, thus requiring only one operator. This has the advantage for recording classes that there is very little in the classroom to draw students' attention to the presence of the cameras. This is often the type of installation selected by institutions that use video for microteaching.

To summarise a rather complicated area: a multiple camera system could be the best option if an institution wants to do a lot of classroom recording but, even for that purpose, it is not the only choice and does require more space, is more expensive and can need more people with appropriate training to operate and maintain it. It is possible to start with one camera and prove the need, before building up equipment, staff and costs.

EDITING

An editing facility allows you to select sequences from recordings that have been made and assemble them in a planned order. If you want to do any more than replay a recording immediately and then erase it, as for instance is common practice in microteaching, then you need some form of editing.

You cannot edit video tape by cutting it, as you can with film or audio tape. With video you edit by copying previously recorded material from one machine to another, assembling the sections you want in the order you want. To do this you need a recorder which has a built-in edit mode, otherwise you get picture break-up at each edit point.

The pause control on some portable recorders acts as an edit button. Non-portable recorders are also available with edit buttons. This allows the simplest form of editing − stop and then start again, with a reasonably clean cut. The stop/start may be to add a new section to material you are in the process of recording, or it may be to copy sections of previous recordings onto one tape. The point is that to do this, you need a machine which has been built for this purpose.

There are much more sophisticated and more expensive editing systems − and they are necessary if anything approaching professional production standards is required − but that level of operation also implies the addition of staff with production expertise, as well as a highly trained technical cadre.

MICROPHONES

The quality of the recorded sound is too often overlooked in a medium dominated by the recorded vision. Classrooms often have poor acoustics, making it difficult to hear students in a recording. The automatic record level in a portable machine means that the microphone adjusts to the loudest sound − a problem if you are recording in a noisy street. The built-in microphone in a portable camera picks up sound all around it − again a problem if you want more than general atmosphere. Sound can be improved by:

(a) Recording in rooms with good acoustics (e.g. with plenty of sound-absorbent material like curtains, carpet, acoustic tiles).

(b) Using external microphones − some recorders can take two so that, for instance, the teacher could be given a lapel microphone, while a microphone on a stand is positioned to pick up the students. Alternatively microphones can be hung from the ceiling.

(c) If good technical expertise is available, it is possible to override the automatic level and to feed the external microphones instead through a sound mixer, which gives much better control over the sound levels each microphone records.

TELECINE

This links a camera to a film projector, so that film can be copied on to video. The same can be done with slides and a slide projector. Telecine systems vary from a simple attachment to very complex machines. Cost and quality also vary correspondingly. Many institutions find telecine a very useful facility, as it enables (copyright permitting) a range of films to be used more conveniently in the classroom. It is also easier with video to add one's own commentary by using the second audio track and this has obvious applications with foreign learners.

In a studio, telecine links into the system so that film or slide inserts can be put into a programme as it is recorded.

7   CONCLUSION

I want to stress two final points.

First, this has been a layperson's guide for fellow language teaching laypeople. It cannot take the place of the impartial technical advice that is essential for any video installation. My intention has been to outline the possibilities so that, by being able to specify what you want to do, you can avoid the pitfalls and select the best options.

Secondly, and most importantly, even with the right hardware and a good range of software, a considerable investment of time is needed to ensure its most effective use. Teachers need to be trained in how to use an unfamiliar resource and they also need time to develop ideas and materials to support the work they do with it. If they are also expected to produce video recordings, however basic, then again they need training, encouragement and time. Investment in video hardware has to be backed up by investment in software and investment in staff, if it is to become an effective aid in the classroom.

8 SUMMARY OF BASIC VIDEO OPTIONS

In order to . . .	*You need . . .*	*NOTES*
Play back recorded video material	(1) a video player (2) a monitor	● *No record facility* ● *Alternative:* *a video recorder/* *player* ● *Choice between* *colour and* *monochrome* ● *Will not receive a* *TV signal* ● *Alternative:* *add RF modulator to* *(1) in order to play* *back through a* *domestic TV set*
Copy recorded video material	(1, 2) (3) a video recorder/ player	● *Could also form basis* *of own recording* *system with addition* *of camera and* *microphone*
Copy off air	(3) (4) a TV receiver/ monitor	● *Alternative:* *if (3) is VHS format,* *it will record and* *play back a TV* *signal through a* *monitor and (4) will* *not be necessary* ● *The addition of a* *timer allows you to* *preset the machine* *to switch on for a* *particular programme*
Record a second sound track	(3) with two audio channels (5) a microphone	

In order to . . .	*You need . . .*	*NOTES*
Record your own video materials	(2, 3, 5) (6) a camera (including viewfinder and lens) (7) blank tapes or cassettes	● *Alternative to (3): a portable video recorder* ● *Another alternative: two cameras (could be remote control) vision mixer control room monitors lights*
Edit video recordings	(1, 2) (8) a video recorder with edit mode facility (9) a second monitor for (8)	● *Alternative is a full editing suite – necessary for any but the simplest editing*
Transfer film or slides to video	(6) (10) a telecine attachment (11) a film projector and/or a slide projector	● *Alternative is a full telecine system (there is a range of choice and quality)*

2 Using a Portapak: Some Practical Advice

CLAIRE WOOLFORD

Claire Woolford teaches English as a foreign language and is also a freelance researcher, writer and presenter of educational radio and television programmes for BBC and ITV. She runs classes in making television programmes at Brighton Polytechnic.

1 WHAT IS A PORTAPAK?

This is becoming an increasingly difficult question to answer as the video industry has moved and is moving very rapidly, so that almost anything that is written will be out of date by the time it is printed. Certainly, if you or your institution are thinking about investing in new video equipment there is a wealth of choice on the market, and you may well find that a low cost colour home video camera such as the one illustrated in Figure 4 may be just what you need.

However, in this chapter we are going to concentrate on the less sophisticated and probably more common black and white portapak equipment that you may have in your establishment. And it is probably true to say that the scripting, organisation and recording procedures for your video material will be intrinsically the same whether you are using black and white or colour cameras.

The two most common makes of portapak equipment are Sony and National Panasonic. As with cars, the equipment is basically the same but varies in detail and, as with cars, you will find enthusiasts for the different makes. As a teacher your main concern is probably that of obtaining the best possible pictures with the least difficulty.

Figure 7 *Using a portapak*

So to the traditional portapak. It consists of three main parts: a camera, a VTR or video tape recorder, and a battery pack or mains unit if you are going to use an existing power source.

THE CAMERA

Although this may look quite robust it is in fact an extremely sensitive piece of equipment and must be handled with care. It has a built-in microphone, but you will find that it is generally better to use a separate mike. The camera is easy to hold and can be manipulated by one person without any difficulty.

THE VIDEOTAPE RECORDER (VTR)

This is basically a machine that records pictures as well as sound. To do this you need videotape, which looks not dissimilar to audio tape apart from the fact that it is wider, much more delicate and therefore needs very careful handling. The VTR is protected by a zip-up case and you are advised to carry it around and keep it in this case as much as possible. The VTR is much heavier than the camera and you will need someone to help you to carry and operate the equipment. Making video recordings is very much a team effort.

THE MAINS UNIT

This has two uses. It can be used to provide mains power, which saves the battery in the VTR, or it can be used to recharge the batteries in the VTR. Sudden surges in the mains electrical supply can blow out any part of the equipment attached to the mains; it is therefore very important to use a variable transformer if the local supply is not dependable.

So those are the three main parts of your equipment. They are delicate, expensive and should always be handled with care.

2 DO'S AND DON'TS WITH YOUR VTR

DO   keep the lid on and keep it in the zip-up case as much as possible. This will protect it from dust.
keep the case zipped up, otherwise someone may pick it up and the VTR may fall out and be damaged beyond repair.

DON'T   touch the video heads except when cleaning them.
thread the tape unless the function lever is at stop and the power is *off*.
touch the surface of the video tape. Handle the tape by its edges as shown in Figure 8.
smoke or eat near the equipment.

If the ends of tapes are crumpled and tatty, cut off the crumpled ends vertically with scissors so you begin threading with nice smooth straight tape.

3 MAKING A TEST RECORDING

To avoid frustration and disappointment you should always test your equipment before going out to make a location recording or before using it with a class. There are few more difficult moments

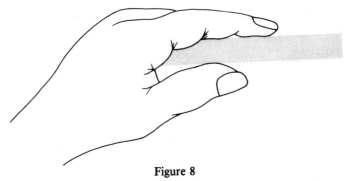

Figure 8

than building your group up to the moment when you are going to use the video equipment only to find that it isn't working properly. Or, having planned a complicated location recording, you find that it cannot be done because the VTR batteries turn out to be flat and you are far from a mains source. It is surprising how often this can happen, so please be warned and make a habit of carrying out the following routine before all recording. It may take a little time at first, but you will soon become used to it.

TEST-RECORDING ROUTINE

Preparing the VTR
1 Check that there is a battery in the VTR. It is located underneath the recorder in a compartment marked *battery*.
2 Check the battery is charged by pressing down *record* at the battery indicator. If the needle is not well into the green area or has not moved at all, then you should recharge or change the battery.
3 Of course, if you are using a mains power source, you need to connect the power pack to the mains and to the appropriate socket on your VTR.
4 Make sure the VTR is switched *off*, while making all connections.

Threading the videotape
1 Make sure the VTR is switched *off*. Remove the videotape from its box and plastic bag and take off the plastic clip.

2 Follow the threading diagram on the inside of your VTR lid and carefully thread the tape.

3 Make sure that you tuck the free end of the tape round the empty spool. The end of the tape should not stick up into the air, as it will catch on the VTR lid when you close it.

4 When you are sure that you have followed the threading instructions exactly and your tape is in exactly the position shown on your VTR lid, switch on your VTR and push the *play* button. The tape should run smoothly from the full spool to the take-up spool. If there is any problem stop the machine, switch *off* and recheck your threading.

5 When you are sure the machine is laced up correctly, then you can zero the number counter. This will show you how much tape you have used. You will also need it when you are looking for particular places on your videotape. In general, the first two figures represent minutes and the third, tenths of a minute.

Connecting the camera to the VTR

Before you start to handle the camera there are two very important don'ts that *must* always be remembered if you want to avoid damaging your camera.

1 *Never* point the camera at a bright light, whether it is the sun or electric light. Inside the camera is what is called a vidicon tube. This is extremely sensitive and the glare from *any* bright light source can burn the tube. This will mean that you will see a dark stain on your pictures. The tube is very expensive to replace.

2 *Never* carry the camera with the tube pointing downwards. Small particles can fall on to the vidicon tube and damage it.

These two points cannot be stressed too strongly, especially when you are showing your students how to use the equipment.

3 Make sure the *camera/TV* switch on the side panel of the VTR is switched to *camera*.

4 Make sure the tracking control on the side panel of the VTR is at *fix*. This may mean turning the knob anti-clockwise as far as it

will go, or turning it until you hear a click. What you do will depend on the model.

The warnings over, you can now connect the camera plug into the socket on the VTR. Do this carefully; there is usually a guide to show you when the plug is in the correct position. Turn the locking collar on the plug until it is tight. This will stop the plug coming out when you are recording. The camera is now connected to the VTR but everything is still switched off. If you look at the diagram of the camera you can see that there is an on—off trigger on the handle of the camera. This means that you can operate the VTR from the camera.

Now:
(i)   Switch on the VTR.
(ii) Press *play* and *record*.
(iii) Press the camera trigger switch once. The videotape should begin to move.
(iv) Look into the camera viewfinder. You should see a red light, which shows you that the machine is recording.
(v)   To stop the machine, press the camera trigger switch again.

Note: do not keep the VTR on standby longer than necessary because it means that the recording heads are running over the same piece of videotape and this can damage the tape and the heads.

But now let's have a look at the camera, remembering not to point it at the light, nor to point it down towards the floor. If you look at Figure 4 you can see that at the front of the camera there are three main parts; the focus, the zoom and the aperture. The lens should be covered with a lens cap and the aperture at *C*, which means that it is closed.

To obtain a picture
You must switch on the VTR and press the *play* and *record* buttons.
Do not press the trigger yet.
Lift up the camera by the handle and point it at the subject

(preferably a still object with some lettering on it). Now look through the viewfinder, and open up the aperture until a picture appears which has good contrast. You can see if the picture is too light or too dark by opening and closing the aperture one stop at a time.

Next turn the zoom ring until the subject is as large as possible. This is called *zooming in*.

Now turn the focus ring until the picture is as sharp as possible. Using lettering as a focus point is a good idea.

Zoom out to the shot you want. The camera is now in focus and you are ready to record.

Note: this process for focusing the camera should always be used:

1 Zoom in as close as you can.
2 Focus on the subject.
3 Zoom out to the shot required.

If this is done, everything between you and the object you zoomed in to, and focused on will be in focus. If the object moves further away, or if you move nearer or further away, the focus will change and the camera will have to be refocused at the new distance.

Recording

You always need to allow about 5 seconds for the videotape to get up speed before you can consider that your recording has started. Failure to do this will give you shaky pictures at the beginning of the recording. If you are recording a person or an actor, tell him to allow 5 seconds after being cued before an important speech or action takes place.

Tell your actor to *stand by*. This means you are about to record.

Cue your actor by dropping your arm and then press the trigger on the camera. The red light should come on in the viewfinder and the reel will begin to turn on the VTR. It is best if another member of the team cues the actor by dropping his arm so that the actor can see it, and as he is cued you press the trigger to start recording.

If this is the first time you have handled a camera, spend some time finding out what it will do. Try zooming in and out on your subject. Then try moving smoothly about with the camera. Move the camera up and down the subject and from side to side. You will be surprised how difficult this is to do at first, but it is important to feel so at home with the camera that it is rather like an extension to your arm. It is thus worth while spending some time familiarising yourself with it. Try to avoid any sharp jerky movements. You will probably notice that the smallest movement of the camera is exaggerated when you replay your pictures. Try looking around the room at various objects and again try moving the camera up and down and from side to side. Also try zooming slowly in and out.

Now press the trigger and stop recording.

Note: if one foot is placed in front of the other the body weight is balanced, and by bending the arm holding the camera at the elbow and pressing it into the chest, the camera is made more stable as the weight is taken off the arm and wrist.

After recording

1 Close the aperture ring, replace the lens cap, and put the camera in a safe place.
2 Press *rewind* on the VTR and wind the tape back to 000 on your counter.
3 Check the tape is not loose. If it is, take up the slack by turning the feed spool anti-clockwise.
4 If you recorded any sound, plug the earpiece into the socket at the front of the VTR.
5 Lift up the eyepiece on the camera.
6 Press *play* and you will see what you have recorded in the viewfinder of your camera.
7 When you have finished watching your recording you may decide to rewind and record over what you have just done. But if you want to keep it you must write down the counter number where you have finished and then you will start to record from there.
8 Press *rewind* and take off your tape.
9 Switch the VTR off and disconnect the earpiece and the camera. Be careful to unplug the camera by the plug and not the

cable, as it is easy to disconnect the wires inside the plug if you pull it out by the cable.

10 Charge the battery. It is important to get into the habit of recharging the battery whenever you can.

Note: make sure that the VTR and mains adaptor are off before you connect anything up. Connect the VTR to the mains adaptor and switch the mains adaptor on (leaving VTR off). The meter should show you that the battery is charging. If your battery is completely flat it may take all night to recharge. It is impossible to overcharge the battery providing the appropriate charger is used (i.e. mains adaptor). If you need to change the batteries then look at the diagram under the VTR and follow it exactly.

The test-recording routine then is to connect up your equipment, make sure it is working and pack it all up again.

4 EXTRAS TO MAKE LIFE EASIER

An external mike

Although there is a mike built into your camera, it is not generally powerful enough to give you good sound quality for such things as interviews or situations where you wish to be able to use the dialogue on playback. The in-camera mike will give you a general ambient sound and will also, if you're not careful, pick up the sound of the lens cap banging on the side of the camera. So it's a good idea to have an external mike which you plug into your VTR and which will pick up sounds more efficiently for your production. There are two basic kinds of microphone; a directional mike which will pick up sound in a narrow range, and an omni-directional mike which will pick up all sounds. Generally for interviewing purposes you will need a directional mike.

A monitor

You can see your recording through the viewfinder in your camera, but the picture is only the size of the viewfinder and so only suitable for checking that you have recorded something. If you want to see more clearly what you have recorded and if you want to show other people your recording then it is useful to have a monitor on which you can watch your programme. This is exactly like a television, except that it has a special socket which you can link to your VTR. You need to make sure that you have the correct leads for both sound and vision and that the switch on the side of the VTR is switched to TV. It is always best to play your videotape back on the VTR on which it was recorded. You will find the picture is better than if you use another machine.

A tripod

Although it is important for you to feel at home holding the camera and moving it about there is little doubt that you will find it a great help to use a tripod. The camera has a hole at the base of the handle and you should be able to screw it onto the tripod. But do be careful because sometimes there is a slight difference between the socket on the camera handle and the screw on the tripod and this can lead to a wobble that will disturb your pictures.

5   TECHNIQUES

So far you've tried to use the camera in a fairly general way. But there are very specific terms for describing the kind of shots you can get through the lens of your camera and the movements you make with the camera. You need to know how to write these down when you are writing a shooting script so that you and your team can follow what you are trying to do.

SHOTS

Since most television shots are of people, shots are descriptions of the way people are photographed, as in Figure 9.

Other shots and abbreviations used are:

Big close-up	—	BCU
Very long shot	—	VLS
General view	—	GV
Point of view shot	—	POV

Close-up which is written on a script as CU

Medium close-up-MCU

Mid shot-MS

Medium long shot-MLS

Long shot-LS

Figure 9

Framing: try to put the eyes about two-thirds of the way up the screen and always leave a space in the direction in which the person is looking (see Figure 9).

MOVEMENTS

Moving the camera from left to right or vice versa is called a *pan*, so on your script you would write 'pan right' or 'pan left'. If you move the camera up or down this is known as *tilt* — and then you write on your script, *cam tilt up* or *cam tilt down*. You have already tried zooming in and zooming out, and again it would be written on your script as 'zoom in' or 'zoom out'. Zooming is not really a camera movement but a movement of the lens of the camera.

6   SCRIPT WRITING AND PLANNING

In this chapter it is assumed that you will have no other method of editing available but the camera and VTR. In this case you have to plan your actual recording very carefully and in sequence, so that at the end of your recording you have a complete programme. This means writing a *shooting script* which will describe exactly what you want to record. You need to decide how long each sequence will be and what you want to say with the programme you are recording.

Then you need to write what is known as a *shot list*. This will define exactly what and who you want to record, and when. Below (Table 4) is an example of a shot list that you could adapt for your own purposes. You need to remember that your videotape is only 15 minutes long and that your battery will only last about 20 minutes. Fifteen minutes may not seem very long, but it is surprising how much you can say in 5 minutes if you plan and time your script very carefully.

Another method of writing down what you want to record is to use a *storyboard*. With this method you can actually draw a sketch of what you want to show. Since videotape is a way of communicating something visually as well as through sound this is

Table 4

Shot No.	Description of shot	Length of shot (approx.)
1	Title: *Injecting a cow*	5 secs
2	GV to establish vet + animal + farm in background	20 secs
3	ZOOM in to vet, CU of him talking	10 secs
4	PAN down to large injection needle	6 secs
5	CU of injection	

very useful as it helps you to visualise what it is you are planning to show in your programme. It is important not to forget that a picture can say as much and sometimes more than words. You should begin to look critically at television programmes. Analyse how they get their effects, how pictures are used in the place of words and how silence and pictures can communicate. On page 48 is an example of a storyboard. Storyboard pads can be bought at stationers.

Planning your script is very important both from the point of view of your equipment recording time and also from the tolerance point of view of your audience or class. Bear in mind that it is difficult for people to see the same picture for more than about 30 seconds, so you should try to do something to vary what they are looking at. Also remember that any change in shot that you make should have some kind of reason or motivation. Don't change shot just for the sake of it; it will look as though you have done just that.

Having prepared your shooting script or storyboard you have to prepare your actual recording. It is a good idea to carry out what is known as a *recce* (from the word *reconnaissance* or *reconnoitre*) before you turn up with your equipment to record a particular sequence. You may think it is a good idea to do this before you spend time on your storyboard.

Suppose, for example, you have decided to make a programme about shopping, for use with your students. You should first of all contact the shop you would like to use and ask the owner or

1. Wide shot of farm and hills to establish where vet is going. Pan along on car, zoom into farm door as vet gets out to meet farmers. Dialogue to set scene.

2. MCU of vet and farmer discussing problem lamb. Zoom into lambs face. Record conversation between farmer and vet.

Figure 10 *Storyboard*

manager for permission to record there. Next you need to fix a mutually convenient date. When you visit the shop you need to decide the best position for your recording, and check that there is going to be enough light. (Although there are low-light cameras available now, most establishments will not have them.) If there is not sufficient light you may have to change your location altogether. Check on the noise levels in the shop. There may be loud pop music playing which will be a distraction you may wish to do without, and you will have to negotiate with the manager.

Once you have set up the recording you need to make sure all your equipment is ready and working and your team of helpers know what each will be expected to do.

As I said in section 3, you should carry out a *test recording* before you go out to check that everything is working and that the batteries are fully charged. It is also vital that you develop the habit of using a *checklist* for your equipment before you go out to do any location work. It is very easy to forget something vital and a whole day may be lost because of it. Below is a basic checklist which you could adapt to your own purposes.

		Checklist
OUT	IN	PORTAPAK COMPLETE
		VTR + zip-up case
		Earpiece
		Empty take-up spool
		Camera, zoom lens
		2 charged batteries
		Charged external batteries
		Mains unit and lead
		1 blank videotape in box
		Carrying case for camera and small accessories
		External mike
		Monitor + leads
		Shot list or storyboard
		Stop watch
		Lighting

If you are recording a scene with actors it is also essential to make a list of the properties you will need, for example a shopping basket, money, a shopping list.

7   RECORDING A PROGRAMME

Once you have arrived at the location and set up all the equipment, you are ready to begin recording. Remember to give the person appearing in front of the camera a cue when to begin. This is very important, because if they start too soon the machine may not be up to speed and you will have to record the shot again. When you are ready to stop recording you will say *cut* and everyone then knows that they have finished recording that particular shot. You should make a note each time of the counter numbers for the beginning and end of each shot. Rewind to the beginning of the shot and watch it on your camera or on the monitor. Check that the sound and pictures are satisfactory. If they are not, rewind and record the shot again. Although this rewinding reduces the battery life it is very important to check each shot or you may get back to your base and find that the whole recording is useless and you have to go back and do it again. A section on common picture faults appears at the end of this chapter.

In-camera editing
It is assumed that you have neither the time nor facilities to edit your material when you return and so you will be using what is known as *in-camera editing*. This means that you must record your programme in the sequence in which you want to show it. It also means that you have to keep a very strict note of the counter numbers so that you know exactly where you want to start recording again.

1   Record your first sequence. Play it back and make sure both sound and vision have been recorded.
2   Find the place on the tape where you want to record the next sequence, stop the VTR and note the counter number.

3 Press *play* and *record* buttons on the VTR (but not the trigger on the camera) and line up your next shot.

4 When you are ready, tell everyone to stand by. Then cue your actor(s) and press the trigger on the camera to start recording. Remember to tell your actor(s) to allow 5 seconds, while the recorder gets up to speed, before any important speech or action takes place.

5 When the sequence is recorded, rewind to the number noted on the counter and play it back to check the recording. If you make a mistake you just rewind and try again. This is the great asset of using videotape. This method of editing is not 100% perfect, but is certainly adequate for most needs.

After recording

Use your checklist to make sure that you take all the equipment back to your base with you. When you have returned, you need to recharge your batteries and report any problems you may have had technically to your technician. Then your programme is ready to be shown.

8 GRAPHICS

If you watch television you will have noticed the titles at the beginning and end of programmes. These are generally called *graphics*. The use of graphics at the beginning and end of your production will help to give it a finished look. A title at the beginning of the tape also allows a teacher using your tape to know immediately whether he has put the right tape on the VTR and that it corresponds to the label on the tape box. Graphics include the title of your recording and any credits or written information you may wish to give during and at the end of the programme. You will need to have prepared any graphics you want to use before you start recording since your first shot should be the opening title. There are certain guidelines that will help you to produce usable graphics:

(i)   They must have a common ratio which relates to the shape of the television screen, and this is basically 4 × 3. This is known as the *aspect ratio*.

(ii)   Many people use black paper and white letraset, or grey paper and black letraset, or some other form of instant lettering for their graphics. As instant lettering is very expensive and also time consuming to use, you can of course use a thick black felt pen on a light coloured card. Make sure the lettering is not too small. You should try out some lettering and have a look at it through your camera. You will soon see what is easy to read and what is too small.

(iii) Don't put your lettering too near to the edge of the card or you will find that you shoot the edge of the card with the camera and this doesn't produce a very good picture.

(iv)   Make sure that the caption is straight before you record it and that the camera is square on to it.

(v)   Below is an example of how to lay out a caption.

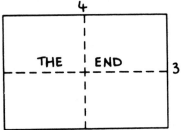

Figure 11

9 LIGHTING

You may not have any lighting equipment in your establishment. Even so, there are certain rules about the use of existing light that will help your programme.

(i)   Never shoot towards the light source, e.g. a window. Have the light behind you.

(ii)   If the daylight is dull inside, switch on any available light source. It will help a little.

(iii) Make a reflector board from a piece of board covered with silver paper. This will help you bounce any available light onto a particular subject.

(iv) Open up the aperture in your camera to let in the maximum amount of light. If you are lucky enough to have a set of lights, you will have another problem when you go on location, as you must have a power source which will take the load. You need to check what this is for your lights. The most common set of lights are known as redheads and come in a large box with stands and leads. They use 800 watts each and can be run off a 13 amp socket. When it comes to placing your lights, basically you need to follow what is called the three point lighting plan. This means that you place the lights approximately as shown in Figure 12 to give a 3 dimensional effect. Lighting is really an added complication and it is probably advisable to concentrate on productions where you are sure there is adequate existing light.

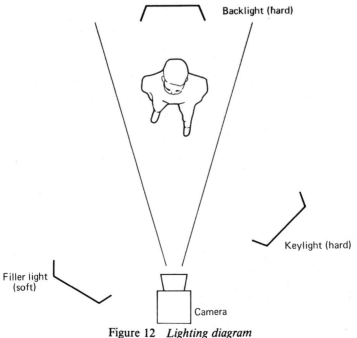

Backlight (hard)

Keylight (hard)

Filler light (soft)

Camera

Figure 12 *Lighting diagram*

10 IT WON'T WORK. WHAT HAVEN'T YOU DONE?

What seems to be wrong?	*Try (1)*	*Try (2)*	*Try (3)*
RECORDING You've switched the power switch on, the recorder doesn't make any sound, and the battery indicator needle doesn't register.	*Using batteries.* Are there batteries in the recorder? Find out by opening the little door marked *battery* on the underside of the recorder. *Off the mains.* Is the adaptor properly plugged in at the mains and into the recorder? Is it switched on?	The batteries may be flat, so try new ones. Check the fuse in the AC adaptor mains plug.	If possible use the AC adaptor.
You've laced up the recorder and played it for a few feet to check that it's laced up properly and it shuts itself off after a few seconds	Did you lace up the recorder with the *play* button depressed? Remove the tape, press *stop* and start from the beginning.	*Using batteries:* When Portapak batteries go flat they die instantly, and don't fade away like a torch battery. So your batteries may have died. Try fresh batteries or charge the ones in the recorder.	Is the tape laced up properly?

The recorder appears to work but the camera seems dead.	Check that the camera cable on the side of the recorder is firmly pushed into the recorder and that the locking ring is secure.	Check that the *Camera/TV* switch next to the camera cable on the side of the recorder is switched to *Camera*.	Have you allowed 30 seconds for the camera to warm up?
Everything seems fine, the camera viewfinder is illuminated but there is no picture.	Is the lens cap off?	Is the aperture control opened?	Are you using the camera in very low lighting conditions? Try pointing the camera at the lightest area in the scene and open the aperture control. (DON'T POINT THE CAMERA AT A LIGHT).
The picture is very hazy and dim.	Try rotating the aperture control through the whole range of settings until the best picture appears.	The light levels in your scene may be too low. Try supplementary lighting.	

What seems to be wrong?	Try (1)	Try (2)	Try (3)
Things like faces and light coloured objects seem unnaturally bright and without detail.	Rotate the aperture control to let in less light.		
The light levels seem all right, but the picture seems very fuzzy and lacking in detail.	Adjust the focusing ring until the picture becomes sharp.		
The picture is sharp, but when you zoom in on an object it goes progressively out of focus.	Remember that at the start of each scene, you must zoom in on the object and adjust the focus. In this way the focus is maintained no matter where the zoom is set.		
Your zoom is on a central object, but you still find difficulty in getting a sharp picture of other objects in the scene.	With low light levels you will probably have to set the focus for each part of the scene. You may have to adjust the focus continually as you shoot.	Use supplementary lighting.	

The outlines of things are unsteady and seem to have sharp jagged edges.	Some recorders need hi-energy tape, others need low-energy tape. Ensure that you have the right sort of tape for your recorder.	
As you are shooting you are monitoring the sound level with the earphone and it seems low and muffled.	Check that your hand is not covering the microphone or the camera.	Move in closer to the object.
		Use a separate microphone plugged into the *mic* socket on the front of the recorder. This takes over from the camera microphone.
As above from ear-phone and a high pitched noise can be heard when using external mic.	Check that the mike is connected properly to the recorder.	

What seems to be wrong?	Try (1)	Try (2)	Try (3)
PLAYBACK – PICTURE Using camera playback you've rewound, pressed *play* and you get no picture.	Check that the *Camera/TV* switch next to the camera cable on the side of the recorder is switched to *Camera*.	Have you let the camera warm up for 30 seconds?	It is possible that although pictures were visible in the view finder while recording, the *play* and *record* buttons on the recorder were not depressed together and so a recording was not made. Try again.
Using a monitor connected to the camera socket on the side of the recorder, you press *play* and no picture appears.	Check that the *Camera/TV* switch next to the camera cable on the side of the recorder is switched to *TV*.	It is possible that although pictures were visible in the view finder while recording the *play* and *record* buttons on the recorder were not depressed together and so a recording was not made. Try again.	
There's a horizontal band of unsteadiness in the picture.	Adjust the tracking wheel on the side of the recorder until the picture is steady.	Was the tape you're playing back recorded on a different machine? Try and play it back on the machine on which it was recorded.	

Symptom	Action		
The picture starts to break up, becomes extremely distorted and then disintegrates into a mass of white pulsating dots.	This means that the recording heads are dirty and clogged up. Test the recorder when you collect it and if necessary get them cleaned there and then. Don't try to do it yourself.		
The edges of things are unsteady and seem to have sharp jagged edges.	The recording may have been made using hi-energy tape in a low-energy machine or vice-versa. Use a compatible playback machine.		
You get no pictures when playing back through an ordinary TV set using a lead from the *RF out* socket on the front of the recorder to the aerial socket on the TV set.	Adjust the TV channel time until you find it. It should be at about 48.	Check that the RF converter is installed in the recorder by opening the little door (marked *RF converter*) on the underside of the recorder next to the battery door.	It is possible that although pictures were visible in the view finder while recording, the *play* and *record* buttons on the recorder were not depressed together and so a recording was not made.

What seems to be wrong?	Try (1)	Try (2)	Try (3)
PLAYBACK – SOUND			
You're playing back through the camera and get no sound.	Check that the earphone is plugged firmly into your ear and the socket on the front of the recorder marked *mic*.	If you used an external microphone it may not have been properly plugged in and you may not have recorded any sound.	
Using a monitor for playback you get no sound.	Check that the monitor has a built-in speaker. Is a sound lead required on your monitor?	Try adjusting the volume control on the monitor.	
Using a TV set for playback you get no sound	Try the volume control on the set.	Try fine tuning the channel tuner on the TV set.	
There is a high pitched noise on the tape.	When recording the external mike was not connected properly.		

In all cases, if you have tried everything, then ask for expert help.

11 DO'S AND DON'Ts

1 *Do* insist on testing your equipment before taking it away.

2 *Do* try to keep the equipment scrupulously clean.

3 *Do* keep the equipment away from extremes of hot, cold, humidity, etc.

4 *Do* ensure that the tape you intend to use is the correct type for the machine you have.

5 *Do* replace the lens cap *every time* you stop recording.

6 *Do* close the aperture control at the end of each recording session.

1 *Never* point the lens at any bright light, including the sun. If you do *you will destroy the camera tube*.

2 *Never* touch the recording heads under any circumstances.

3 *Never* leave the equipment unattended without switching off the power and ensuring that the equipment is in a secure place.

4 *Don't* subject the recorder or camera to any shock. *Don't drop it!*

5 Touch the tape itself *as little as possible*.

6 *Never* drop the batteries. Hold them singly.

The author would like to thank Joanna Tait, Mike Harvey and Janette Graham for their suggestions and advice.

3 'Talking Heads' and Study Skills Programmes

MARION GEDDES

Marion Geddes has worked in educational radio and television in India and Ethiopia and as a teacher and teacher trainer in many other parts of the world. While working at the British Council English Language Teaching Institute she planned three of their teacher training films.

Nowadays there are many programmes to train overseas students in the language skills necessary to follow a course of academic study at a university or college in an English speaking country. As long as lecturing remains a common teaching technique in higher education, a major aim of these study skills programmes must be to develop the student's listening skills so that he can learn to listen with confidence and take useful and efficient notes while he is listening. Many students don't understand as much as they could: in their concern to understand every word that is spoken they panic. They need to be trained to recognise not only what is important and relevant in the speaker's discourse, but also what is irrelevant and therefore does not have to be perfectly understood. A student who can learn to select and reject with confidence will listen with greater understanding.

Typically such training and practice is given with the help of material recorded on audio tape. This was the case at the British Council's English Language Teaching Institute (ELTI) in London. However, when the Institute acquired video equipment (a portapak camera, videotape recorder and viewing monitor), staff were quick to try recording new listening and note-taking practice material on video as well as audio tape. Video could obviously add variety to classroom presentation. More importantly, the addition of the visual element could allow us to record lecture material where the speaker referred to visual information − perhaps a diagram or set of formulae, a map or a model, or something written on the blackboard.

Even where the speaker did not make use of visual information of this kind, we still felt that there was a case for making video recordings of lectures. Paralinguistic features such as gesture and facial expressions should help the students' comprehension. And video recordings could present students with a better simulation of reality without the student or the teacher losing control. The lecturer could still be stopped and his words repeated; the teacher could still know in advance what the lecturer was going to say and prepare supplementary materials and exercises. But on video the speaker's presence was more immediate and real than on audio tape. The student could listen to an embodied rather than a disembodied voice, a 'talking head' instead of merely a voice.

A minor consideration in favour of making such recordings, but one that should not be forgotten, was that they were an easy introductory exercise for staff wanting to familiarise themselves with the new video recording equipment. In making recordings, staff developed confidence in handling the equipment and learned basic technical points about shot framing, size of aperture in relation to the amount of light in the room, the positioning of the microphone, and the need to check and remember all the details necessary for a technically successful recording.

The reaction of students to videotaped lectures was extremely positive, both in the early experimental groups where we used our first talking heads, and on subsequent courses when students were exposed to other types of video material as well, and so video was less of a novelty.

Having talked a lot amongst ourselves about the possible importance of paralinguistic features in helping students' comprehension and the contribution of video in this respect, we were interested to observe what with hindsight seemed obvious. Because the students were busy taking notes, a lot of the time they were not looking at the screen and so missed many of the gestures or facial expressions that we felt could have been significant in helping comprehension. Why then did they prefer this form of presentation? Both from students' comments and from our own observation, it was clear that one important function of the video screen was to provide a strong focus of attention. As students looked up from their notes, their eyes had something relevant to focus on − the person they were listening to. An audio tape recorder does not provide a meaningful focus in the same way. It was also clear that the picture on the screen gave authenticity and reality to the voice and helped give the student confidence that after his language course, when he found himself in a university lecture hall, he would be able to follow the lecturer there too.

Those brought up in the best traditions of television production may react to the notion of one camera shot lasting perhaps for as long as seven minutes. Manuals on television production give similar advice on the question of duration of shots: 'Held too long, attention will wander. Having assimilated the visual information, thoughts dwell upon the sound . . . The limit for most subjects is about 15−30 seconds'.[1] But when making recordings of lectures it is important not to think in terms of programmes that must be visually attractive. One is concerned with simulating reality. In real life the eyes of a lecturer's audience will wander away from him to other members of the audience, or to features in the physical surroundings. But these wanderings are individually and personally motivated. Different camera angles and changing shots are external motivations, forcing the audience's attention to switch from front view to profile, from close-up to long shot. Changing camera shots can be visually distracting. Hold the same camera shot and let the student's thoughts 'dwell upon the sound' − and let him find his own distractions in the classroom he is sitting in.

MAKING RECORDINGS

Talking heads are simple to make. One member of staff can work alone, allowing only a little more time than he would if the recording were to be made on audio tape. At ELTI a sizeable library of recordings was built up quite quickly. Most recordings were made either at ELTI or at the house of a member of staff or of the lecturer. Only occasionally were recordings made of lecturers speaking to a real audience of students. This was mainly because of the great length of the material that resulted and the problem of extracting and editing pedagogically useful chunks from it. It is also time consuming to take equipment to an unfamiliar place, where one has to make sure in advance (usually by an earlier visit) that there are suitable power sockets, lighting, acoustics and so on.

When making recordings of talking heads we concentrated on 'lecturettes' − short lectures that were self-contained in the sense that the speaker was able to present and conclude an argument or description or discussion without speaking for more than five to seven minutes.

Lecturers ready to talk on a wide variety of topics were found amongst friends or staff − experts on economics, sewerage, history, urban planning, physics, veterinary science, etc. Each lecturer was asked to prepare a talk on a topic within his academic field that would last not longer than five to seven minutes and to try to talk to the camera as he would to a live audience of students, from notes if that was what he was used to. He could use a blackboard or overhead projector or any visuals that he wanted as long as he gave us advance warning. We also asked him to lend us print material related to his topic. When it came to making the recording, we would try to put the speaker at ease by assuring him that the recording could be erased and either forgotten or made again, as he felt necessary. We always made a simultaneous audio tape recording to use in transcribing the lecture and for possible use in the language laboratory. This saved us the bother of making a recording later from the audio track of the video tape.

Here is an example of how one ELTI video lecturette was exploited.

EXAMPLE: RURAL URBAN MIGRATION

An urban planner, who also lectured regularly on a planning course for Latin American students (our target audience), gave a seven minute lecturette on rural−urban migration. After the lecturette had been recorded, a transcript was made by a teacher. The advantage of a teacher doing this rather than an audio typist is that the teacher becomes very sensitive to the speaker's language while transcribing, and ideas start forming in his mind as to ways in which the material could be exploited.

An article describing some other ELTI materials[2] gives a list of options for work related to video material. Some of these were used with the rural−urban migration lecturette: oral work in the language laboratory; reading of related material for notetaking, for detailed comprehension, and for skim reading; and seminar-type discussion.

Below are extracts from the teachers' notes for the unit on rural−urban migration that was developed from the video lecturette. It is clear from these that the talking head is only one part of a long unit integrating several skills. What is important from the point of view of materials design is that the video lecturette is the starting point. Until the recording has been made one cannot know what language is going to be produced and how the speaker is going to organise his thoughts and ideas. The options open to the materials designer are in large part dependent on this language and organisation.

EXTRACTS FROM TEACHERS' NOTES FOR UNIT ON *RURAL−URBAN MIGRATION*

Materials

The following materials are available:

1　Preparatory reading text: *The Growth of Urban Centres*
2　Statistical table: *Urban/Rural Population of Developing Countries*
3　Videotape lecturette, with transcript: *Rural−Urban Migration*
4　Four language laboratory drills, with tapescript
5　Supplementary reading text: *Urbanisation and Political Protest*
6　Skim-reading exercise, with worksheet: *Rural−Urban Migration and Metropolitan Development*
7　Four parallel reading texts: *Kuala Lumpur, Lima, Manila Bandung*

Suggestions for exploitation

1 Preparatory reading:

   1.1 Introduce essential vocabulary (rural, urban, migration, developing country, etc.).

   1.2 Ask students to prepare group summaries of the text on OHP transparencies.

   1.3 Ask two or three group representatives to present their group's summary to class.

2 Statistical table:

   2.1 Help students to verbalise information presented in table, with reference to preparatory reading text.

3 Video lecturette:

   3.1 Play once through, with students taking notes.

   3.2 Go over students' notes, replaying tape and rewinding as necessary to draw attention to rhetorical markers, linking devices, etc. Build up model notes on OHP. Establish framework of lecturette (see laboratory drill 4).

   3.3 Replay lecturette, with students taking notes for a second time.

   3.4 Prepare students for laboratory drills.

4 Language laboratory drills.

5 Supplementary reading text:

   NB The way the writer has organised his text provides an interesting parallel to the way the speaker organised his lecture.

   5.1 Establish with the students what common assumption is going to be refuted by the writer (paras 1–9).

   5.2 Ask half the class to read paras 10–15, while the other half reads paras 12–18.

   5.3 Get the students to exchange information about what they have read and then orally anticipate what the writer's conclusion is.

   5.4 Ask the students to complete the reading of the text at home.

6 Skim-reading exercise:

   NB This text gives the students background information about four cities, one of which they will read about in (7).

   6.1 Ask the students to complete the skim-reading exercise within five minutes. Check their worksheets orally, perhaps exploiting it for oral work on comparisons, etc.

7 Parallel reading texts:

   7.1 Distribute the 4 texts equally among the students, giving each student *one* text, for home-reading and study.

   7.2 Conduct a seminar-type discussion on *Urban Squatters and Violence*, based on the information and evidence provided by the parallel reading texts. (Notice that two texts claim that squatters are a major contributing factor to the increase in violence in urban centres, while two texts claim that this is not the case.) Encourage the students to use the language practised earlier in the language laboratory drills, and to refer to all that they have read or heard about while working on this unit. They may also be able to draw on their experiences in their own countries.

CONCLUSION

A recording of a 'talking head' presents a better simulation of reality than sound only, and helps students' confidence. It also provides a focus of attention for the student while he is listening and allows him to make use of paralinguistic features. Variety is introduced in the presentation of listening comprehension material and a lecturer can make explicit reference to visual material. The recording is easy to make in terms of staff time and expertise, and it can be a starting point for the design of a unit of material integrating other skills.

NOTES

[1]Millerson, G. *The Technique of Television Production*. Focal Press, 1972.
[2]Sturtridge, G., McAlpin, J., Harper, D., *English for Academic Purposes Materials Development*, in Cowie, A. P. and Heaton, J. B. (eds.), *English for Academic Purposes*. BAAL/Selmous publication, 1977.

4 The 'Witness' Activity: Group Interaction through Video

EDDIE WILLIAMS

Eddie Williams has taught in France, Cyprus and Malta. He has been involved in teacher-training in Italy and Portugal and he is currently working in materials development, teacher training and direct language teaching at the Centre for Applied Language Studies, University of Reading.

1 INTRODUCTION

The activity that this chapter will describe is one of the simplest ways of exploiting video. Despite its simplicity however it is an activity that takes advantage not only of the salient features of video as a medium of communication, but also of the group dynamic inherent in a classroom situation. As with many simple techniques however, its success depends upon the appropriacy of the material, and also the classroom management of the steps by which the material is exploited.

I intend to develop the above points by describing the basic steps in the activity, then discussing what sort of material might be appropriate. Finally I shall consider the merits and limitations of this activity.

2 THE PROCEDURE

As its label suggests, in a 'witness' activity, the learner simply reports what he or she has witnessed on the screen. The steps in the classroom are as follows:

1   Introduce the video sequence. This should be very brief. I sometimes say no more than *Watch this*. However if the video sequence has been filmed in a location familiar to the class, then one might say something like *Imagine you were standing in the (name of building/room). You looked out of the window and this is what you saw*. At this point the class are not told that they will subsequently be asked to act as witnesses.

2   Show the sequence straight through without pause or replay.

3   After the sequence has been watched, the class may be asked a few general questions about what they saw, for example *how many people were there, what were they wearing, what happened first, what happened next*, etc. These questions should be kept to a minimum. Their purpose is two-fold: first they give the learners an idea of the kind of points they will need to look for in their reconstruction of the sequence, and second they usually lead fairly quickly to disagreement, and a degree of personal involvement in the activity.

4   Ask the class in small groups to prepare a reconstruction in note form of what they saw (it is preferable if each person in the group has his own copy of the group reconstruction). Again this tends to produce a great deal of discussion since individuals tend to differ on how many people were involved, or what the sequence of events was. At some points their reconstruction may have to allow for alternatives if no agreement can be reached.

5   Each group then reports to the class as a whole their reconstruction of the sequence. Sometimes there may be no need for each group to go through its entire reconstruction, but simply to comment on or modify the account given by the first group. For the sake of clarity the teacher may here note the points and the alternatives on the board.

6   Show the sequence again with pauses and replays as necessary; each person now confirms or corrects his own account (hence the need for each viewer to have his own copy of the notes).

7   Finally the viewers may as individuals or in the small groups write out a 'witness account' of the sequence.

3 APPROPRIATE SEQUENCES

One should perhaps not be too dogmatic if one has not (as I have not) explored all the possibilities of the 'witness' activity; experience so far, however, suggests that silent sequences exploited in this manner are more engaging if they depict an incident that one might in real life reconstruct (for example for the police or for friends). There should therefore be an element of the dramatic or unusual in the sequence. Examples are a handbag snatch, an accident, a fight, an attempt to move a heavy object, etc. There obviously has to be a clear visual narrative that can be 'read' without the need to understand what might be said. On the other hand the episode should not be so simple that it can be reconstructed without giving rise to any discussion.

From the technical point of view the sequence will be more plausible if it is filmed from one position; there should be no cuts, or close-ups, and characters should not walk out of the picture, but should exit through doors or round corners. In fact it is preferable if the camera is kept at a fixed focus some distance from the action so that the viewers see the whole scene as they might have done in real life. For the same reason the sequence should be a continuous sequence in 'real time'. In order not to overburden the memory the sequence should be fairly short, perhaps no more than two minutes (though much depends on how much is actually happening); in addition it is preferable if there is no significant action at the very beginning so that viewers may get a chance to 'tune in' to the situation.

From what has been said it is obvious that such a sequence is one of the simplest to film oneself. It requires only one camera, no sound, and no editing. All that is required is a group of reasonably co-operative actors; as there are no close-ups and no sound they do not need to be especially competent in this respect.

4 MERITS AND LIMITATIONS

The main language production in this activity obviously takes place in the discussion phase. The language used is of two types: first, the language of reporting, i.e. telling what happened – narrating – and describing; it involves much use of past tenses and time sequencers. Second, the interpersonal language of the discussion, involving agreeing, disagreeing and expressing degrees of certainty. For the discussion stage to be effective learners will need reasonable competence as far as the vocabulary involved in reporting the particular sequence is concerned.

In terms of ways of agreeing/disagreeing and expressing doubt/certainty learners need not be highly sophisticated; the activity will give them a chance to practise what they know and the teacher may introduce one or two more (for example, *You might be right, but . . ., I'm not sure about . . .*); this is best done at the end of the session, since it tends to break the fluency of discussion if done in group work.

The activity capitalises on two aspects of classroom video. First, it capitalises on the fact that video can present movement in real time – still pictures or slides can hardly bear comparison since by freezing action in time they direct the viewers' attention to what is happening in that particular instant. A listening input (with tape-recording or teacher reading) can only give a one-dimensional account which involves a great deal of preselection of what is described; this again tends to focus the learners' attention, rather than leaving them free to select and interpret.

Second, the activity capitalises on the classroom situation: the small group discussion generates interaction and motivation. The uncertainties or disagreements mean that the learners select for themselves the points on which they wish to focus their attention in the second viewing. The fact that this focusing is done by learners rather than the teacher clearly increases their personal involvement. Whether this increases learning is a moot point, but it certainly does not detract from it.

Third, the involvement of the learners with the activity both in discussion and viewing means that the teacher is not under continuous pressure to 'keep everything going'. The groups do this themselves, leaving the teacher free to act as a language informant or manager of the activity as the need arises.

The limitations of the activity are those imposed by the nature of appropriate sequences. The language of reporting, agreeing/ disagreeing and expressing disagreement are clearly only a small part of the whole range of language use. The language skills involved are mainly those of listening and speaking; writing occurs in the note-taking, and it may be felt that to provide a written reconstruction is a rather clumsy way of introducing consolidation. However these limitations seem to me to be outweighed by the fact that the activity is enjoyable, motivating and provides learners with a chance to exploit what they know through real communication with each other.

5 *Video for Analysis and Correction of Learner Performance*

STEPHEN HICK, GARETH HUGHES, CHRISTOPHER STOTT

Stephen Hick, Gareth Hughes and Christopher Stott are co-associates of York Language Training Associates. All three have wide experience in teaching and designing materials for English for occupational purposes in the UK and abroad.

Video has an important role in monitoring the performance of language learners involved in communicative activities. The questions that we shall discuss and attempt to answer are:

why we should choose video as a recording medium
what we should record
how we should exploit the recording

There is obviously considerable overlap between these areas, but a consideration of the benefits of video in the most general sense is a reasonable starting point.

WHY VIDEO?

With video, we now have a superior recording medium capable of recording both sound and picture. Rather than asking the question *Why use video?*, we should perhaps be asking ourselves whether we have good reasons for deliberately excluding the visual element from our recordings of communicative activities. In the same way that sound recording provides a truer recreation of spoken language than pen and paper, so does video provide a truer recreation of a communicative event, where paralinguistic features form an integral part of the communicative process.

Teachers of language have become increasingly aware that their job is to teach communication rather than language in a narrow sense. So video's ability to capture the total context — paralinguistic as well as linguistic, together with the physical environment — is extremely valuable. Video also offers a greater vividness which can contribute positively towards helpful analysis of the learner's performance. For suggestions and corrections to be meaningful and effective, the learner needs to relive the moment when an error or difficulty occurred. Because video is better at evoking the total context, the learner is more likely to locate the mental process that produced an error or difficulty. People today are also more attuned to televised recording than to sound only.

Against this, however, we must acknowledge the fact that video is still a relatively expensive medium. In most teaching establishments access to video equipment is limited, and criteria as to why or when to use video are needed. Furthermore, video recording equipment is much more cumbersome than sound and is more demanding on operator time. Therefore, recording short periods of speaking on an impromptu basis is obviously more practicable with audio tape.

WHAT TO RECORD

In general, we would prefer to record interactions rather than exercises; that is to say, periods of speaking which have a communicative intent, not solely practice of language items. Whereas, during practice, correction is normally made on the spot, in an interaction we believe that correction should not normally intrude; the case for recording is, therefore, stronger. Preference for video, in particular, as the recording medium will be most likely when communication depends on a visual element, for example:

when visual aids are being used
where instructions are being given which involve subsequent

physical realisation
where a demonstration or tour is taking place
when we are interested in seeing people's reactions to language
used by others in discussion.

Video may also be preferred where the camera can help to highlight
communication breakdowns, whether the participants are visible to
each other (as in the above examples) or not (as on the telephone).
The breakdown may be revealed by something as obvious as a
wrongly carried out instruction or as subtle as a facial expression.

We will later look at the recording of three of the types of activity
mentioned above in more detail. However, prior to that we need to
consider the third question we raised earlier: how do we exploit the
recording?

EXPLOITING THE TAPE

It may be that a recording is being made to check performance in
areas of language usage which have supposedly been learnt.
Corrections can be made and remedial work devised. The tape will
also reveal what has been well learnt. Given that video provides
more of the total context than other media it is not very productive,
in our experience, to concentrate too much on errors made at the
word or sentence level. It is better to use the video recording as an
opportunity of seeing language in its wider communicative context.
Video can show up discourse features and more general
behavioural aspects of communication, such as the organisation of
information in a speech and the appropriateness of reactions to
others in discussions. The recording can, of course, also provide
meaningful context for sentence-level points of grammar, so that it
may well be possible to treat some such errors effectively.

An alternative use for the video recording (one that does not
necessarily conflict with the first) is for diagnosis. The recording
can effectively reveal situations where the learners do not have the
means to communicate what they want to. Again, video is
especially good at showing up wider communicative problems, such

as the inability to interrupt at a meeting, or to make it clear that you want to move on to a new point in your speech.

As well as there being different reasons for making the recording, there are various ways of conducting the playback session. Traditionally, playback analysis has been dominated by the teacher who stops and starts the tape as he sees fit. Although he may invite question and comment from the learners, essentially the learners perceive such sessions as passive ones. Whilst such an approach to a recording may be of value to the teacher for diagnostic reasons, we would question its value to the learners.

First, as we have said, their role is a passive one and we do not see passivity as being conducive to effective learning. Secondly, the 'errors' dealt with by the teacher often derive not from the learners' competence but from their performance. Learners are often quite capable of correcting such errors themselves.

If we call the above correction model teacher-controlled, then the next possibility is for an analysis of the tape which is jointly controlled by teacher and learners. There are various ways of achieving this. The teacher can retain overall direction by instructing particular learners to watch out for particular points as the tape is played back. Thus, the teacher might ask for someone who has problems with a grammatical structure to spot its occurrence and comment on the accuracy of its use. Functional points can be treated in a similar way through appropriate delegation. Alternatively, the learners can be asked to raise points about the whole. Although the teacher retains the power to make comments and is likely to remain the dominant member of the group, such joint ventures help the learners to become more active, more involved and more self-critical as a group. However, the teacher's sensitivity to frictions within the group and to any problems of loss of face arising from discussions such as this is extremely important in determining the kind of comment that can be invited and from whom.

At the other end of the continuum, the learner-controlled model for playback analysis will only involve the teacher participating when requested to do so. One way of achieving this is for the teacher to leave the room for the playback until the group is ready to recall him. This sort of approach is in line with teaching methodologies which see the teacher in terms of a helper or counsellor. It is obviously unlikely to succeed with learners who have not been asked to think for themselves before. Teaching a group how to learn takes time and we would expect this to develop as the course develops. Once acquired, however, the sensitivity to language and communication which learner-controlled playback requires can be used for continued learning after the end of the course.

The correction model to be chosen will, it goes without saying, depend on the style of the rest of the course and on the purpose of the playback session.

As examples of the use of video for the purpose of playback analysis, we have chosen three different types of language activity that we have recorded for teaching purposes. The first involves inter-group communication centred on the relaying of instructions. The second is concerned with intra-group discussion and role-play. Thirdly, we will consider the use of video for the analysis of spoken monologue.

EXAMPLE A

INTRODUCTION

The first example describes an instructional game using Lego building bricks. Learners are divided into groups for the purpose of designing structures, devising written instructions for their assembly, and relating those instructions, orally, to the other groups of learners, who are required to build the structure. The part of the activity where oral instructions are given and executed is filmed.

Although the language content in our example is at elementary level, entailing simple instructions and notions of location, dimension and colour, the same methodology can be used for different tasks and refined for different language levels. In fact, it can be used for any task that requires a sequential assembly process, be it Lego, Meccano or a carburettor.

In terms of classroom management, the video can be operated by the class teacher. The camera is pre-set on the group to be filmed and the playback analysis can follow the activity directly, without the need for the teacher to make an independent review of the tape.

ACTIVITY

After the class has been divided into two groups (although there can be more), each group is provided with an identical kit of Lego building bricks and a base board. There should be about 15–20 bricks of diverse colour and shape, easily identifiable by such terms as small, blue, square, and so on. Each group is asked to design a simple structure, such as a house or a chimney, within a time limit. When the groups have agreed on the design of their structure, they produce a set of written instructions for the construction sequence (e.g. (1) Place the small yellow brick on the board. (2) Put the square brick on the yellow brick . . .). The teacher's role at this stage may be no more than advisor to the two groups.

Each learner is then made responsible for the relay of a certain number of the instructions to the other group. The actual relay of information is done orally and not read from the written instructions. Filming begins at the stage when the relaying of information starts.

First, group A act as instructors to group B, the builders. Each member of A in turn comes across to B in order to relay the instructions he has been entrusted with. The builders are free to ask questions of the instructor. It is worth noting that learners new to this kind of activity will probably find themselves in all sorts of disarray, particularly the builders. Nonetheless, this can be a useful area of language analysis in the ensuing playback session. On completion of the first structure, the positions are reversed and the builders become the instructors for their own design.

At the analysis stage, we are concerned with assessment of the success with which the instructions have been given, received and carried out. The correction technique found useful for this activity is centred on playing back the performance of each instructor and the response of the builders. Frame-by-frame analysis can highlight the actual points where mistakes in the building have been committed. Learners will be quick to point out these mistakes. The teacher can direct the playback to probe the reasons for this:

Was the instruction wrong?
Was it badly phrased?
Was it not understood for another reason?
Did the builders not understand a reasonable instruction? Why not?

In general, teachers will be interested in linguistic errors and the learners in communicative failure. The use of video for analysis and correction provides an excellent means of reconciling these two concepts in a realistic manner.

EXAMPLE B

INTRODUCTION

Whereas the previous example provided an example of video use in which the communicative content of the activity can be fairly well predicted, this example, recording a simulated business meeting, can do no more than provide ideas about how to approach the playback. This is because the communicative range possible is so wide that the teacher can never be sure of what exploitative possibilities the video recording will produce. The language level of the participants needs to be intermediate and the interaction must be open-ended.

Because of the open-endedness, the teacher is likely to find himself with a much longer tape than in the first illustration. He will need to decide if it is best to play back just a part of the tape and, if so, which part. He will also need, if he is directing the analysis stage, to decide what aspects to concentrate on. This requires good notes on the tape's contents, which in turn necessitates either a second teacher or a learner to operate the camera during recording while the teacher can make notes; or time for the teacher to view the tape before the learners see it. It should be remembered that the second option is very time-consuming: it always takes longer than you think. Another possibility is to pre-set the camera and use just one camera shot, but that is uninteresting to watch and close-ups are often very revealing.

Simulated business meetings provide valuable practice for learners of English for business purposes. Such meetings can be used as tests of performance and for diagnosis of communication problems. A popular format is the role-play. There are variations to this format but the essential component is that participants have roles (defined to a greater or lesser extent) imposed upon them. This kind of interaction can produce valuable language practice but it is, in our experience, rarely successful in producing convincing role-play *per se*. For this reason video recording has drawbacks in so far as it is such a good recording medium that it exposes bad acting and distracts from the language. This conclusion is at least valid for groups of mature, adult learners.

ACTIVITY

The following is an example of one way of getting round the problems associated with role-play. It is to provide the participants with the problem but not with the roles. The learners are given a project which requires discussion but which draws on individual talents and experience for its solution. The problem needs to be suited to the group: in this case, an upper-intermediate level group of five managers from different national subsidiaries of a multinational company was given the task of developing a sales campaign. At one stage, part of the group was required to present proposals to the rest of the group for discussion and decision. Both the presentation and the discussion were recorded. Here we shall just look at the discussion stage.

In this example, different members of the group were asked by the teacher to look out for particular points. The teacher remained in class for the playback and participated in the analysis. A major area that was ear-marked for analysis was that of *suggestions*. One member of the group was delegated to spot any examples of suggestions being made. When an example was located the situation was summarised, the speaker's intention was ascertained, the force and impact of the utterance were discussed, and the correctness and appropriateness of the linguistic exponent were considered. In this way, a list of the suggestion forms used in the meeting was drawn up together with other forms which would have been more appropriate at certain times.

The important part of this technique lies in embedding the language point to be analysed (and corrected if need be) in its full context. The recording helps the speaker to recall his intention at the time of speaking and it helps gauge the effect of the utterance on the listener(s). Without the picture it is also more difficult to identify speakers and follow the discussion, e.g. seeing where a participant has failed to break in to the discussion. It is also important for the teacher to recognise successful language use, which is not so evident as unsuccessful use, and to identify covert errors. A covert error may exist in the avoidance or non-use of certain words or structures, so the playback analysis should aim at increasing the learners' range of expression as well as correcting what they actually said. A covert error might also lie in the actual utterance not having the meaning or force which the speaker intended: hence the importance of knowing the speaker's intention. Finally, the error might be the listener's in misinterpreting what was said although, superficially, he appeared to understand. Sensitivity to language, therefore, is an essential for the teacher and it is to be developed in the learner.

Apart from specific points spotted by the group or the teacher, the playback analysis also produced some general impressionistic comments from the group. One of these was that the discussion was very slow. It was decided that, apart from the problem of finding the right words, one reason for this was that people were tending to try to say too much and that the course should pay attention to ways in which people could put their points across simply yet effectively: a general language technique rather than one specifically related to English.

The playback thus produced some hard points for follow up, and some work on forms of suggestion, together with some thoughts to bear in mind when participating in the next discussion. The playback in this case also produced some valuable discussion practice in itself.

EXAMPLE C

INTRODUCTION

As our third example of video for playback analysis we have chosen the recording of a single learner giving a talk. As well as being a monitor, the camera can substitute as an audience for the single learner. The camera should, therefore, be operated with a view to recording wherever the speaker directs the audience's attention, if the playback analysis is to be effective. This is particularly important where the talk involves the use of visual aids, such as in many business or technical presentations. A good zoom lens is essential and the camera must be operated throughout.

ACTIVITY

Our example concerns an individual of intermediate level from middle management in an international company. The learner had to present five arguments to justify the adoption of a particular management procedure. The aim was to practise the movements inside a piece of discourse – introducing a point, closing a point, moving on to the next point. The learner chose to reinforce the main arguments with OHP transparencies on which all information was in written form.

During the playback session the learner was asked to focus mainly on the language used to indicate transition from one argument to the next and on the relevance and effectiveness of visual aids. The playback analysis was seen as a joint evaluation by the teacher and the learner. With this particular learner, the lack of formal markers in the discourse made it very unclear as to which point was being made; the confusion for the listener/observer was further compounded by the fact that a change of topic did not coincide with changes in what appeared on the OHP screen.

Such problems are common in presentations of this type and the visual element in the recording assists the learner in his own analysis of his performance. Lack of eye contact and stiff posture often make delivery very tedious. The presence of physical gesture and stress and emphasis in linguistic presentation can contribute significantly to the effectiveness of the speaker. The video can also assist the learner in his evaluation of the impact of both layout and language content of his visual aids. Too many words on an OHP transparency can reduce its effectiveness. Excluding superfluous language is often a skill which needs developing by this type of learner.

The structure of the presentation above was relatively simple — five points whose order was not particularly important, and the OHP transparencies presented information in exclusively verbal form. The video is of equal value where more complex talks are given, involving main and sub-topics. With visual aids giving numerical, tabulated or graphical information, deficiencies in language referencing devices are more readily noticeable if the visual element is present in a playback analysis.

In order for video activities to be successful, it is important that they are developed as an integral part of the learners' course work. The language content must refer back to work previously done and, if necessary, be pre-taught for the purpose of the video recording and analysis. The analysis itself will be the source of further class-room work and, if appropriate, will lead to the next video activity. From a technical point of view, the teacher must learn to use the camera proficiently, for a badly shot recording will not satisfy an audience who, visually, will make comparisons with the sophisticated products of television and the cinema. It is important that video lessons are well planned, especially where the availability of video recording equipment is strictly limited and for the purpose of analysis maximum use is to be made of the tape. The need for good organisation applies also to the conduct of the playback session itself. Whatever the approach selected, the aims of the session must be clear in the minds of both teacher and learners. The danger is that the playback can easily seem an anticlimax after the interaction, and concentration lags to the detriment of learning.

Finally, the nature of the course will have implications for the playback model of correction used. During an extensive course there is time to develop the learners' critical awareness of what is seen on the tape, and the method of learner-controlled correction can be particularly valuable. However, for learners untrained in this technique, such an approach may only lead to confusion and a waste of video facilities.

6 Student Video Production

ELAYNE PHILLIPS

*Before becoming an EFL teacher, Elayne Phillips taught
drama in schools in the UK. She has given several
workshops in drama for English language teachers in
Britain, Denmark and France. She is now teaching at the
Bell School of Languages, Norwich.*

One of my main concerns in language teaching is to provide
circumstances that maximise student participation and creative
involvement. Video is one of the most exciting fields into which this
energy can be channelled.

Here I do not propose to sing the praises of video recordings as
sources of information, stimuli for discussions, instruments of
provocation, illustrations of specific language items or as pure
entertainment, although I do not wish to deny that they can be all
of these. My interest lies in video production − not by a band of
professional folk, nor by a handful of theatrical teachers aspiring
to celluloid immortality, but by the students, with the students and
for the students.

The beauty of video lies in its simplicity. Anyone can operate a
video camera, given the minimum amount of instructions and the
freedom to experiment with it. The same applies to the video tape
recorder and monitor. Being able to use and control the video
equipment is the first basic step towards creative and confident
video recording. Rewards are rapid and the feeling of achievement
accumulative. There is nothing like success as the most highly
motivating factor.

Another attractive feature of video recording is the almost
instant replay that is possible. Mistakes can be rectified, changes
made, new elements added or removed, and the overall quality

improved. The knowledge that umpteen retakes are possible until the perfect shining product emerges dissolves inhibitions and boosts confidence. Nothing so easily thwarts the elusive creative spirit as the 'one piece of paper and that's your lot' syndrome, knowing that if you make a mess of your first attempt, you're not going to have a second chance.

The third most appealing aspect of video (so obvious that it is often overlooked) is the universal familiarity of television as a means of communication. Few homes are without a set. No student needs an introduction to it and communication is far more effective when it is both visual and oral.

So basically video is a simple effective tool that can be used again and again to achieve a variety of ends in a variety of ways. How then can the making of video recordings be used as an effective means of language learning?

Let us assume that students who have chosen to follow language courses are basically interested in communicating, most of all with each other. It is up to us as teachers to provide them with readily available facilities and a conducive environment where they can best express themselves according to their individual and group needs.

The most essential factor is to put the video into their hands by first leaving the choice of subjects, themes, and treatment of each video film entirely up to them. This may initially seem like a frightening degree of freedom, but with careful guidance (guidance, not control), huge amounts of encouragement and ample room to experiment, clear aims and directions will emerge.

1 SETTING UP

Each member of the group should familiarise himself with the equipment and its operation as soon as possible, so that any technological mystique surrounding machines is utterly dispelled. By being allowed to experiment with the video camera and videotape recorder, rather than *your* giving *them* instructions and watertight demonstrations, your students are more likely to discover for themselves the range of recording possibilities that video has to offer, and thereby develop physical and imaginative dexterity through practical application. Posing a problem or series of problems inevitably sets off a steady language flow; only here the problems are real and hence the language becomes realistically contextualised. Don't tell them where the plugs are or how to connect up the various components. Let them find out for themselves how to zoom in and out without losing focus and how to fade shots in and out for various scenes. The less you show them what to do, the more they will find out for themselves. You will find that gradually one student and then another will discover new tricks. In every group of students there is at least one 'technician' – someone who appears to be endowed with more practical knowledge than the others. This student will be only too willing to pass on his newly acquired expertise. And so it goes on – those who manage to sort out various difficulties explaining to those who can't. The various vocabulary items and expressions should be taught as and when they are needed.

A simple test to check that the recording procedure and relevant vocabulary have been fully assimilated is to ask each student (obviously not all on the same day, but at intervals throughout the early part of the course) to demonstrate to the rest of the group. If it can be arranged in your school or college, they might even give demonstrations to other groups who have not used the video equipment before and are anxious to do so.

2 SETTING OFF

Having given the students the camera, you then take it away. This may sound a somewhat drastic measure and not far removed from that of taking candy from a baby. But this is only a temporary measure.

PRE-RECORDING ACTIVITY:
SETTING UP A STILL SHOT

(Note: the camera is not used at all during this activity.) Each student takes it in turn to set up a still shot. He selects three or four other students and arranges or poses them as if they are part of a scene from a film. In other words, he directs them. For this he needs to use fairly precise language in order to arrange his characters physically and also to explain the mood and content of the scene. This is best done away from the rest of the group with only the teacher present to help out with any language difficulties. When the shot is arranged, the director gives the order to *freeze*, and the rest of the group then try to work out what the scene represents and make suggestions as to what happened before the *freeze* and what might happen after it. Simple props such as guns, hats, flowers, newspapers, etc. add an intensifying element of realism to such shots, and false noses, glasses and wigs enable students to hide behind a disguise, which they may need to do at the beginning. Encourage each student to try this activity by asking for volunteers as ideas occur to them. In this way each student has the opportunity to experience what it feels like to be a director.

This activity not only produces plenty of language but may stimulate the imagination and provide ideas for video recordings. Many of our recordings have stemmed from such activities.

DISCUSSION

At this point it is a good idea to pause for discussion and ask your students to consider the variety of social encounters and situations that are suitable for video recording and are feasible, given the limitations of the rooms available, the 'actors' and costumes, props, furniture, etc. Ideas will vary considerably from group to group, but whatever suggestions are put forward they should be given serious consideration so that your students take responsibility for their own productions right from the beginning.

POSSIBLE SUGGESTIONS

1 Interviews (*a*) of students
             (*b*) of staff
             (*c*) of famous personalities
             (*d*) at a press conference

Figure 13

Figure 14

Figure 15

2 Domestic scenes
3 Business scenes
4 Social scenes
5 Banking, shopping procedures, etc.
6 Scenes involving high drama, usually of a tragic nature
7 Crime stories
8 Comic situations
9 Documentaries
10 Fantasy productions based on popular myths
11 Commercials
12 Recordings that demonstrate specific linguistic structures
13 Demonstrations: cookery, playing a musical instrument, showing origami, etc.
14 Discussions, particularly of a controversial nature
15 Ambiguous situations designed to provoke questioning language
16 Mime to which students watching the recordings can add the appropriate language
17 Stories (narrated or acted out)
18 News items (read out by students playing newsreaders)
19 Recordings involving toys, objects, sound effects
20 Science fiction programmes

These are just some of the recordings that have been suggested by students over a number of courses, most of which were followed up with varying degrees of success. Now let us look more closely at one of these suggestions.

THE INTERVIEW

Recording an interview is perhaps a simple and safe introduction to the video production world, particularly if you have your one and only camera in a fixed position. It can also be carried out with a minimum of preparation and each student can in turn take the various roles of cameraman, interviewer and interviewee.

First set up the 'studio'. The person to be interviewed sits facing the camera. Spotlights are directed towards him from either side. (We always use adjustable 500-watt spotlights and these make an enormous difference to the quality of the image). The cameraman then focuses and fixes a close-up shot on the well-lit face of Mr X who is seated against a plain, preferably contrasting, background. The person interviewing Mr X stands behind the cameraman, slightly to one side, and the microphone is suspended between Mr X and the interviewer. In this way Mr X will appear to be looking at the camera, when in fact he will be looking slightly above and a little to one side. All these preparations may seem a little pedantic and you may find a superior and alternative system, but I do believe in insisting on a high professional standard in order to achieve the best visual image and quality of sound that the equipment and the production crew are capable of producing. If the image is furry and the sound muffled, any interest aroused will rapidly evaporate.

But to return to the interview. With a new group an interview can be a useful way for students to find out about each other, the countries each comes from, their interests, etc., as well as giving everyone the chance to experience what it feels like to be behind camera, on camera and off camera. (Incidentally, the questions asked by the person interviewing need to be spoken clearly as he is never on camera. They can be prepared in advance, but not learned by heart as the spontaneity and freshness will be lost.) Each interview need only last a few minutes, and each time everyone changes role (cameraman, Mr X and interviewer) until everyone has had a turn. Should you have a reluctant group (a rare phenomenon) you might like to put yourself in the chair and be interviewed first. Never force anyone who does not wish to be interviewed.

If everyone in the group knows each other fairly well, they could adopt entirely new personae, in order to make the interviews more interesting with totally unexpected answers. Another variation is to arrange all the students (apart from cameraman and Mr X) in a semi-circle facing the person to be interviewed, but off camera. Each student can then ask questions as and when he thinks of an idea. Mr X turns to face each questioner in turn with the result that we see Mr X from a variety of different angles without having to alter the camera position. This activity could well lead up to an improvised press conference of a famous personality:— someone who has just arrived at an airport, or has just received an important award, or has been released from prison, etc. Such an improvisation needs very little preparation, previous role-play or drama experience, can be very demanding on the students, involves everyone and often produces very exciting results.

One of our student groups chose to do a series of interviews of famous (but fictitious) sports personalities. The student that volunteered to have a go at being the interviewer proved so successful that he interviewed everyone. This was particularly interesting, as in normal class discussions and role-play exercises he was extremely shy and withdrawn as well as being inarticulate. On camera he was transformed. All the other students each chose a sport and a personality. A few facts about each one's life and achievements were given to the interviewer before the interview. Each sportsman also wore the appropriate sports gear (one even turned up to class in full riding gear), and each interview was directed by a different student.

It was decided that the interviewer would be on camera for each scene and hold the microphone. The 'directors' were free to handle their interviews in any way they chose. The only stipulation I made was that each scene should have its own unique visual treatment (as regards setting, shots, action, etc.) so that the whole production would not become a series of boring interviews with two people sitting opposite each other. This necessitated a good deal of discussion and rehearsal before the actual recording. There was a definite competitive feel in the air as each director tried to work out the most original way of recording his interview. One even had the couple wandering about in the woods outside and the camera shooting them through the window. This was made possible by the use of a zoom lens (which we use for nearly all our work), a long lead on the microphone, a glorious summer's day, and the students' ability to make themselves heard above the deafening birdsong. One student was interviewed while being massaged and another as he was carried off a football pitch after being injured.

Another group wanted to make a documentary of the school and decided upon a series of interviews. This time the famous personalities were the staff, both administrative and teaching. This programme (made two years ago) has since been repeatedly shown to new students as a way of introducing the staff to them and to make them feel at home. The students who made the documentary established a good relationship with the staff they interviewed, particularly in discussions afterwards. Questions were prepared in advance by the students but none of the interviews were rehearsed before recording so that they could be as fresh and as realistic as possible.

With projects such as these (which often develop from the simplest of beginnings) I am constantly made aware of the exciting possibilities of video recording and production.

3 THE PRODUCTION PROCESS

There are naturally no hard and fast rules about the way one goes about making video programmes, nor about the time spent on each stage of the process. Everything depends on the students you are working with (numbers, levels, temperaments, group dynamics, etc.), the time available, the equipment and space, as well as your own personal style and method of approach.

Usually I work with small groups of students (between six and twelve in number), of *mixed* ability, experience and level of language, who choose to make video programmes as one of the option courses available to them. They are drawn together by common interest rather than by level of linguistic proficiency. Some groups work together better than others (as with all groups of students) but a co-operative spirit is encouraged from the beginning. In video production everyone has to work together as a team, playing interchanging roles as members of the crew or cast. During most ten-week terms we have two 1½-hour sessions per week (30 hours total), and in some terms three, but video courses can and have been run even in the very shortest of summer courses (10 hours in total). It helps to get started immediately by making a short and simple recording in the first or second session.

If you are working on a two-sessions-a-week basis, allow one session for preparations and discussion and the following session for recording. Students seem to like working in pairs (cameraman and director) and each pair take full responsibility for their production. They need first to decide what their programme is to be about and then to explain it to the rest of the group. Discussion may well promote several changes of plan. Those taking part must be quite sure of what is expected of them, and any costumes, make-up, props, furniture, special lighting or sound effects should be prepared in advance (certain articles may have to be borrowed or bought). To begin with, encourage the students to keep their ideas simple, to plan a production lasting no longer than five minutes, and to work out the dialogue through improvisations.

Recording takes place in the following session. The video equipment, lighting and stage are set up in accordance with the director's instructions, and then there is a run-through of the scene so that the cameraman can get some idea of the moves and dialogue. The fact that the first run-through is basically technical takes some of the pressure away from the actors going through the difficult business of their first rehearsal in front of the rest of the class. Make a short test recording to ensure the microphone is working and the vision is being recorded. Many a beautiful recording has been lost when we have omitted to do a test, and then found that the microphone had not been plugged in, nor the recorder switched to *camera.*

Then the real recording begins. Introduce words like *action, take 1, cut,* etc., as well as a few gestures vital for silent communication during filming. These will help each director to give clear instructions to his cast and crew. At the end of the first take (or rehearsal), play the tape back for everyone to see and invite criticism, first from the director and cameramen, then from the actors taking part and the 'film critics' (i.e. the rest of the class) who have been watching. Ask them to suggest ways in which the scene might be improved.

Contrary to what one might assume, students on the whole are less inhibited when improvising in front of a camera than in a classroom situation. This is largely because of the degree of concentration required to work in this medium and the importance that students place upon their performance because it is being recorded. They soon become aware of the need for certain theatrical techniques (keeping one's face towards the camera, using exaggerated gestures and facial expressions, the need for articulate speech and sometimes voice projection, sensitivity towards grouping, etc.) as soon as they see themselves on television. Give them some practice in such techniques as various needs arise. The high standards of technique and acting set by television today ensure that most students have an inbuilt and highly sophisticated visual sense.

Video is an ideal medium for dealing with linguistic error analysis. Mistakes will often be realised and even rectified by the students who made them. *Seeing* themselves in role-play situations, students will often become aware of the appropriateness or inappropriateness of the language, register, attitudes and gestures that they have used.

But to return to the production process. After the first recording and after any necessary linguistic, spatial or content changes, record the scene again. When it is played back, encourage your students to think of ways in which the scene could possibly be made more interesting visually, orally or dramatically for the viewer. Ask questions such as: does it end well?; could any of the scene be cut?;

is it too slow at any time?; do we need any more light?; does anything need to be added?, etc.

Beware of taking over from the director. He is responsible for his production, and he must decide how many takes are needed and how many changes there are to be made until he is satisfied. Very rarely will a director insist on more than three takes and sometimes he is perfectly happy after one. As soon as the director feels that enough rehearsals have been carried out, he should inform everyone that the next take is to be the final one. This often works wonders.

A time limit helps for recording, and a 1½-hour session is very often long enough to complete a recording (of 3 or 4 minutes). This sense of completion, of having achieved something, and produced something tangible is very important.

4　HOW MANY STUDENTS?

The number of students you have in your class will obviously determine the organisation of that group. If you are fortunate enough to work with groups no bigger than twelve, then you can involve them all in the same production process. If, however, you have thirty or even more in your classes, then you would be well advised to split them up into groups of ten or so. In this way one group can be recording and the other two can discuss ideas for recording, perhaps putting these ideas down on paper. Then in rotation each group takes turns to record, while the other two are preparing − at times becoming involved as extras in crowd scenes, or as film critics when the recording is completed and shown.

5　TO IMPROVISE OR NOT TO IMPROVISE?

Being asked to improvise a situation may seem a terrifying and tall order even in one's own language. This is very often the case until one has actually tried it. Simple, undemanding improvisation exercises can be used to build up this confidence and ability. Try setting a situation, them improvise it, and go through the same situation with a script. It is often found that whether the script has been learned or is read aloud, much of the freshness and realism is inevitably lost. This exercise can be recorded for the students to see for themselves. The mistakes in language made during improvisation are not, to my mind, of sufficient importance to risk losing the vital ingredients of realism and spontaneity – and besides, one learns by making mistakes.

For the first half of one video course (in a ten-week term) we based all our recordings on improvisations. Then the students asked if they could work with scripts. These they wrote themselves and learned by heart. The results were interesting. At first they kept very closely to the scripts, worrying about missing out the odd word and losing much of the vigour and pace of their previous performances. Gradually they began to improvise around these scripts until we were back where we started – improvising completely. At least they were satisfied that improvisation was, for them, the better of the two methods. Here one must bend to the needs of the students. If careful scripting and direction gives a firm basis of security, then stick to scripts; but if students prefer the freedom of improvisations, then help them to become talented improvisers with plenty of practice.

In general, with any group of students making their own video one should be prepared to move with them, helping them to reach their individual and group aims.

Working with different groups of students over the last two years, I have noticed a very interesting and curiously parallel development in the nature of the productions. To begin with, the recordings were very wordy, full of heated arguments, debates and interviews where students almost seemed afraid to pause for breath. Then towards the end of each course the amount of dialogue dropped to a bare minimum. One group even produced a totally wordless programme of seven scenes as their grand finale. I was beginning to question my role as a language teacher and to wonder how I could justify a video course as a vehicle for maximising language production. Visual communication had taken over. Atmospheric music and sound effects had replaced the spoken word. The scenes were full of students pacing up and down and sighing pensively, with mysterious smiles and meaningful gestures. Everything became mood and feeling, actions enigmatic and ambiguous. However, in order to achieve all these effects the various directors of these 'silent movies' had needed to use extremely complex and precise language to explain exactly what they required of their actors and technicians. So absorbed had we become in the films themselves that we were unaware of quite how much language we had been using to get there.

6 INTRODUCING PROGRAMME TOPICS

Not all the ideas come from the students, nor can they be expected to without at least a minimum amount of infiltration now and again. By this I mean the drawing of the student's attention to certain aspects of video of which he might not otherwise be aware, and which could fruitfully be assimilated into his own video programmes. So, during a ten-week course I would probably introduce some half-a-dozen topics. Here are a few examples.

Symbolism Bringing into the class a selection of symbolic objects or pictures such as a rose, a key, a cigar, a dead rat (*not* a real one), a knife, a torn-up photograph, etc., and inviting comments and suggestions for inclusion in programmes.

Music and sound effects Playing different pieces of music and asking students to conjure up scenes. Playing different sound effects and asking them what they are and how could they be used in programmes. We have on occasion made our own sound effects.

The use of different shots Discussing the effectiveness of close-up shots, wide angle, low-level and high-level shots, etc.

Costume, make-up, etc. Demonstrating the use of various disguises and make-up.

Violence in films This is only one of a series of themes which are useful for discussion, backed up by the showing of appropriate film clips.

7 SHOWING FILM

It is of course highly relevant to show students excerpts from films (those that are commercially produced, and video productions by former students), and to encourage them to see as many films as possible. This increases their visual and critical awareness as well as widening the range of possibilities for their own video productions. Perhaps it is wise to refrain from showing the video programmes made by other students until they have made several of their own and have reached a certain standard. Nothing is more daunting than to flaunt the end-of-term products of past video students (who have had the benefit of a whole term's production experience) in the faces of new and very inexperienced students. It may act as an incentive, but is more likely to have the reverse effect.

8 WATCHING FILM

Try to make the activity of film-watching an active rather than a passive one. This can be done in a variety of ways, for example:

(a) Setting questions (on paper) for the students to answer and discuss in small groups.

(b) Asking the students to look out for certain elements and to comment on them.

(c) Inviting criticism and ways of improvement.

(d) Stopping the film from time to time and asking what has happened so far.

(e) Stopping the film from time to time and inviting suggestions as to what might happen next.

(f) Turning the sound right down and asking the students to imagine or make up the dialogue.

9 STUDENT VIDEO PRODUCTIONS

(a) *Scenes from a language school*: interviews and exchanges between students and staff. A documentary.

(b) *Sports personalities*: a series of interviews of 'famous' sports personalities.

(c) *Newsreading auditions*: several students attempting to audition for the post of newsreader, making every mistake possible, and I should add, deliberately. This has been a useful recording to show to other groups who then attempt to rectify the mistakes.

(d) *Horror story*: a story written and read by a macabre student with a background of suitable graphics and horrific noises.

(e) *The Fortune Teller — a love story*: with a happy ending and some tear-jerking piano music played by one of the students.

(f) *No man is an island*: a wordless seven-scene film about the loneliness of modern man and his attempts to overcome it.

These are just a few of the programmes that have been made over the last two years. Others include recordings of mime sequences, various domestic situations that invariably result in horrific arguments, crazy quiz games, innumerable visits to doctors, hospitals, and psychiatrists, demonstrations, recordings of revues and plays performed by the drama groups, and even an attempt to make a recording of a recording being made.

10   FUTURE PLANS

In the future, depending on the inclinations of the various students choosing to do video courses, it would be interesting to make recordings for specific use as teaching material with other groups: for example, mime sequences, ambiguous situations, and even language teaching programmes with the students teaching simple structures. Students love looking at recordings of their fellow students and learn much more from them than recordings of people they feel no sympathy with.

Working with video is a process of endless experimentation, where one is discovering new tricks and new possibilities all the time. The more one works with video the more one realises just how enormous the potential is in terms of content, technique and flexibility. But the main reason for making recordings is for the students — for their language development and to encourage a creative and co-operative spirit among them. The preparation and necessary language work that goes into the video production process is of far greater validity than the end product. The end product is for the students. It is their motivating force and their reward, very often more highly prized than any exam or teacher's report, since it is all their own work.

7 Redlands Television: a Simulation for Language Learning

GILL STURTRIDGE

Gill Sturtridge has taught in many parts of the world and has worked on numerous teacher training courses overseas. At present she is working in materials development, teacher training and direct language teaching at the Centre for Applied Language Studies at the University of Reading.

The objective of this media simulation is to stimulate learners into using the foreign language while working on a common task. Putting together a TV programme provides the opportunity for the natural integration of listening, speaking, reading, and writing skills. The students have to read instructions and details of news. They have to prepare announcements, captions and scripts, and above all, communicate with each other as they decide what to include in the programme and how to record it. The final video recording that the students produce will not be a polished sophisticated programme such as we see on our own TV screens, but the true value of a media simulation lies in the process of making the recording, not in the quality of the end product.

When video is used in the language classroom the student usually has the role of viewer. It is sad that his possible role of video producer is so often overlooked, for student production of video recordings has a valuable contribution to make to language learning. Students are able to use a camera and recorder with minimum help and training and prove to be careful users of expensive equipment.

REDLANDS TELEVISION

This particular media simulation provided the students with the task of producing a 15 minute news programme called *Reading Round Up*. The students were employed by an imaginary television network, Redlands TV. The programme was named after the town and university of Reading where the students were studying and the network was called Redlands after a local street; it is a good idea to give local names to the programme or ask students to choose the names.

The group were allowed the whole morning, 3½ hours in all, to produce the programme. However, where there are timetable constraints the simulation could be divided into shorter blocks of time, perhaps using three or four class hours to put the programme together. Producing the programme on one day with a deadline has the advantage of motivating the students to work at speed and gives an urgency to the whole production.

The students were provided with one portable camera, a video tape recorder with playback facility, a second machine with editing facility and a monitor. Having the facility to edit the film was a welcome luxury but the simulation could equally well have been done without the second machine. The students were also provided with plenty of grey paper and letter stencils, pens, scissors and glue to help them with any captions they decided to use. To save time they were provided with an audio cassette recorder and some pre-recorded cassettes of selections of suitable music from which they could choose a signature tune for the programme and background sound.

To fire the imagination of the group there was also a large collection of objects such as plastic fruit, toys and hats which could be used in the recording.

Students are very inventive and tend to make use of anything or anybody when making a programme, but giving them a collection of objects helps to produce some excellent ideas in the desert of the classroom.

In the making of *Reading Round Up*, very little decision-making was left to the students at the initial stage. With a more experienced group and with more time available, it would have been possible to give the students a completely free hand in the choice of material and in the production of the programme. However, this was the first time the group had handled video equipment and the length of the programme, the length of its component parts and what each student had to do, were clearly specified. The teacher provided most of the input for the programme and assigned role cards to each of the 18 students in the group. The input consisted of memos, messages, audio tape recordings and letters. These provided the outlines of stories for the reporters to follow up and suggestions as to where they might find further news or information. The role cards told each student his job in the production team, who he was responsible to and the deadline for the programme. The two key roles were those of *Producer/Presenter* and *Technician*. These two students were asked to come in early to discuss their tasks and the tasks of those in other sections. The Technician was given basic instruction on how to handle the camera and equipment, but the teacher remained at hand throughout the production to make suggestions and help where necessary. When the rest of the students arrived they found their classroom had been transformed into a TV studio. A printed notice *Redlands Television* was on the door and the room was set out with six tables clearly labelled with the names of the sections. As each student came in he was given his role card, a badge marked *Redlands TV* and the name of his section so that he could go direct to his table. The tables were the home-base for each section.

They were:

1	*Production*	The Producer, The Technician and Graphic Designer
2	*Foreign News*	The Foreign News Editor and two reporters
3	*Home News*	The Home News Editor and two reporters
4	*Advertising*	The Advertising Editor and two copy writers
5	*Viewers' Requests*	The Requests Editor and two researchers
6	*Sport*	The Sports Editor and two reporters

Each section had an in-tray containing specific instructions for their section in the form of written memos and news stories. These were the raw materials for the programme and provided students with a wide variety of ideas for stories which the reporters could follow-up if they wished. The information about possible stories came in various forms including TELEX and pre-recorded cassettes of reports. Students went to the *Reuter Agency* in the Language Laboratory to listen to these cassettes and take notes on the reports. (Such a news agency could also be set up with a single tape recorder if no laboratory is available.) Some of the news stories were fictitious and involved students and teachers.

MEMO
TO: Producer
FROM: Welsh Home Affairs Reporter, CARDIFF
DATE: 23.4.80

There are reports here that the Welsh language is to become compulsory as a second language throughout Britain and will be taught in all secondary schools.

Investigate. Suggest interview with Mr Ed Williams.

The reading, sorting and discussing of news stories involves a great deal of language work. Even if students sometimes lapse into their mother tongue during their discussions they are still working *on* and talking *about* the production of the foreign language. There are, for example, script writing and interview preparations to be done; most reporters feel they want to perfect their questions before recording the interview. Those students in charge of the *Viewers Request Section* have to make summaries of the letters they receive and do research so they can give brief clear answers. The students in the Advertising Section select from a range of *sponsors requests* for advertisements and write the slogans and produce the advertisements for the products. (*Redlands Television* is a commercial network!)

In this particular group the producer sent a memo to all the section suggesting that everyone be seen on the screen during the programme and even the most camera-shy of the 18 students appeared in some role or other. At least five modelled the hair styles in the advertisement for *Fifi's Hair Salon*.

The programme opened with the producer writing the words *Reading Round Up* over a map of Britain which the group had found. There followed a series of short interviews and news flashes interspersed with advertisements. An Ideal Home Exhibition was open on the University Campus at the time the students were making the programme and the reporters from the *Home News Section* took the portable camera and recorded interviews with visitors and stallholders. This exploited the potential of the portable camera and gave the students an opportunity to do real interviews. A similar activity could be used overseas where those interviewed would not speak English but what they said could be translated, either at the time of the interview or with voice-over later. The *Advertisement Section* made full use of all the props provided. In an advertisement for the *Taj Curry House* the group used puppets and toys to portray a typical family at supper. They moved the heads as they spoke the dialogue they had written. Here is the dialogue exactly as they showed it to the teacher before they started recording:

Mother (a fluffy dog)	Would you like another dumpling darling?
Father (a large teddy)	Definitely not. I'm fed up with this stuff.
Mother	Oh dear. Fuzzy – won't you eat up your peas? Can't you hurry up a bit?
Fuzzy (a puppet snake with a mop of hair)	Oh, I hate this stodge everyday the same. Let's have some change.
Father	Yes, Fuzzy's right. Let's have some change. Let's go to the Taj!

Fuzzy   Yippee! That's the big idea.
                                     Let's go to the *Taj Curry
                                     House*. Off we go!

The teacher suggested some alterations and rehearsed the three students briefly.

Simulations are never a soft-option for the teacher but a media simulation makes even greater demands upon him as he has the additional job of technical advisor as well as language advisor. Though students soon learn to use the video equipment they often need some suggestions about graphics or ideas on how to make the programme more visual. There is certainly a great deal of language work for the teacher, as reporters need help with pronunciation or need a script to be checked. However ragged or unprofessional the finished programme may be, the students inevitably have a sense of achievement when they see the results of their hard work. They are also critical of their own performance in the foreign language and come back to the teacher with specific language questions, on which future classes can be based. Thus student use of video is not only an excellent opportunity for language practice but also has long term value as a motivating force.

8 *The Use of Video Films*

DAVID KERRIDGE

David Kerridge has been teaching English as a foreign language for the last ten years, mainly in Paris. While working at the Régie Nationale des Usines Renault he took part in various seminars on the applications of video in the EFL classroom.

This chapter will deal with the classroom use of the authentic and semi-authentic video material which can be obtained by hiring, buying or occasionally copying off air.

By authentic material we mean any unscripted (but probably edited) television/video programme which has *not* been made for learners of English. The only difference between this and semi-authentic material is that the latter is scripted. For example, under these headings any comedy, entertainment or training film would be semi-authentic, while any discussion programme would be authentic. For the sake of simplicity, we will use the phrase *authentic material* to cover both types throughout the chapter.

Although, literally speaking, any English language television programme is potentially usable as an English language teaching aid, it is advisable to identify the three categories most often exploited in the classroom so that later suggestions regarding their exploitation may be as concrete as possible.

The categories are:

news/weather/advertisements
documentaries
films (training or entertainment)

The use of non-EFL video material in an EFL classroom poses many difficulties. But we do not believe that these difficulties differ greatly from those encountered while using authentic taped conversations or newspaper articles. The difficulties may *seem* greater (because of the linguistic and technical sophistication of sound and image) and this means that we must train ourselves to judge these materials with a certain rigour (see below: Section 1 on choice of material). An example of the difficulties encountered could be a news broadcast commentary where the camera image has only an indirect relationship with the words of the commentary. This does not mean that the news broadcast is *per se* unusable, but it does suggest that the broadcast should be analysed carefully before any exploitation of it.

Before going into detail about the choice and exploitation of video material, we think one general remark about the role of video is appropriate here.

Video material is not some sort of pedagogical short cut (as the language laboratory was once thought to be − with disastrous results) and is not qualitatively different from any other teaching aids that exist; neither does it provide a reason for less preparation of lessons − rather the contrary, as will be seen.

1 CHOICE OF MATERIAL

As we have mentioned, choice of material is a difficult subject pedagogically, but also logistically.

First of all, teachers have only the BBC's magazine *Radio Times* from which to choose off-air material for copying*, or television companies' voluminous catalogues, or one-off previews as bases from which to choose materials for hiring or buying. This situation, logistically, often results in a library full of unused or underused off-air video cassettes, or video cassettes chosen from catalogues, both taking up valuable space. Although this situation is financially less dramatic for the off-air material (which can always be recopied) it is nevertheless far from perfect in terms of time and materials invested. This problem has no magic solution, but there are ways in which it can be ameliorated.

* But see Chapter 11 for information about copyright restrictions.

Pedagogically, it is important that the potential of any bought or hired authentic material be clarified before the material is acquired. Anything chosen *only* because the buyer likes it or it seems suitable or its subject matter seems relevant may well be deficient in several vital aspects.

Therefore, before commitment, a buyer will have ideally viewed the material and have studied the transcript (the full text of the dialogues/conversations). Then, by asking himself some of the following preliminary questions, it should be possible for him to make at least an informed guess as to the suitability of the material:

(a) What does the material teach? (if a training film)
(b) Is what it teaches (apart from English) relevant to my learners? (if a training film)
(c) Can it be integrated into the course system?
(d) What relevant ancillary activities can be devised?
(e) Can it be broken into sequences?
(f) Can it be exploited with more than one target group of learners?
(g) Will the material have a primary or supportive role in the course?

and, not least important,

(h) Do I (the potential buyer) like the film?

You may have noticed that none of these questions begin with *how*? When choosing material the relatively simple *what*? questions must be asked and answered first. The more complex *how*? questions regarding the actual exploitation possibilities of the material come later. The reverse could lead to a lot of time spent preparing perfectly good lesson plans and then exploiting them to the wrong target audiences.

Most of these *what*? questions are, to some degree, connected with course integration. Just as the blackboard or tape recorder has a role in the classroom which changes according to level and group, etc., authentic video material also has a role which changes according to circumstances.

To take a hypothetical example: suppose we have a 10 minute

cartoon training film on basic accounting procedures in a small company. Our learners are accountants working for large multi-national companies and are in the UK to learn the language skills necessary in their jobs. They need to function with their peers and superiors at a fairly high level.

We could make the following suppositions: professionally, the level of the film would be too easy for them; they might not like cartoon films; perhaps small-company accountancy has very little relevance to multi-national accountancy, etc.

Role: this material doesn't seem very relevant to these learners' needs. However, if it has any validity for this group, we might consider its role as introductory or for the revision of vocabulary at the beginning of the course.

The point to note here is that the role the material plays should fit the needs of the target group of learners, and not vice versa.

So the role changes. And, just as we do not buy or record taped discourse without having a fairly precise idea as to its eventual classroom role(s), neither ought we to procure authentic video materials without having similarly precise ideas.

However, having said this we find it extremely difficult to draw up any global criteria for choice. This is because all the variables surrounding different English courses must be taken into account if we are to be fairly sure of obtaining a reasonable pedagogical mileage out of a particular piece of material.

In choosing materials we have to ask ourselves the relevant preliminary questions, then link the answers to the needs of our target audience and the constraints of the course. At the present time, this process is still at the informed guesswork stage. Apart from this guesswork, there are of course additional factors to help us although these stem more from linguistic insight.

Length, subject matter and the role of humour are three of the factors to be taken into account.

Length and subject matter: material does not always have to be short. Under certain circumstances and with certain groups a 2 hour entertainment film or a 50 minute documentary on divorce may be extremely valid learning aids.

Humour: the sort of humour found in much authentic material illustrates how easily mistakes can be made. For example, non-visual humour based on the rather byzantine English class system, while amusing for natives, often finds learners frustrated and baffled — see section 3 example 2. (This serves only to underline the necessity for a certain sensitivity to the socio-cultural background of the learners.)

If the above ideas on the choice of material seem too general, it is probably because they have not been written with one learner in mind. Instead, we have tried to make them relevant to a multiplicity of learning and teaching situations. Thus it would be unwise to be too prescriptive.

2 EXPLOITATION OF MATERIAL

The role of video material in the classroom is, in all senses of the word, central. It is the principal purveyor of information. This does not mean that the teacher is peripheral or redundant. But it does suggest that his role has to be redefined according to these new circumstances. This redefinition is not very different from the changes necessary when tape recorders first became standard classroom equipment.

In general terms, the most important change is that the teacher's *interpretative* role has been cut to a minimum. Let the video do the work. During a tape-recorded listening comprehension exercise, you would not repeat a difficult phrase immediately for the benefit of a class which has not understood it. The same principle holds good for the exploitation of video material.

We hope that you will find the following practical classroom hints useful:

1 Give learners a preliminary non-technical introduction to the equipment, to de-mystify it.
2 During this introduction, explain that learners will not necessarily be expected to understand all that they see and hear.
3 Explain that only those parts of the sequence that reinforce/teach the aims of the course will be exploited.

4   During the sequence running time sit with the learners, not beside the television, thus giving the impression of participation.

5   If appropriate, encourage learners to operate the equipment themselves during the lesson.

6   For the smooth running of the exploitation, note the counter numbers of the sequence beforehand.

7   The exploitation of authentic video material has far less need to be predictable than that of EFL course material. Variety needs to be the keynote.

The next three hints concern timing or pace:

8   Authentic video sequences seem unsatisfactory tools for certain structural-type exercises (e.g. learners having to put a speaker's words into reported speech) which necessarily involve the teacher continually stopping and starting the equipment.

9   From various classroom observations it seems that about two hours is the maximum that should be devoted to the appropriate number of showings of any particular video sequence plus ancillary activities.

10 It is difficult to revive interest in a second session of a once exploited sequence simply by changing the ancillary activities and the aims of the exploitation.

Authentic material by its nature is often much richer than material designed for EFL purposes. This means that pedagogical aims of any particular exploitation must be carefully defined beforehand, and rigidly adhered to. Without this prior definition, learners (and teachers) may easily allow lessons to degenerate into general discussions which, although often interesting, have little relevance to the course aims.

Bearing in mind that authentic material in the classroom is a fairly recent phenomenon, these general 'rules' have been written to be adapted to suit circumstances. In that way we hope a more generally applicable pedagogy of this sort of material will slowly develop.

Story: this sequence is one of the funniest in the video, and visually it is fairly obvious what is happening. Beckett is awaiting an important visitor with whom he has an appointment. A man comes into the office. Sandra, mistaking him for the expected visitor, shows him in to Beckett without introducing him. (In fact he has come to inspect the radiators.) Another man (Robbins) arrives a few minutes later and Sandra refuses to let him into Beckett's office, not believing him when he claims, rightly, that he is the expected visitor. He leaves angrily, followed by the radiator inspector. Sandra and Beckett have an argument. The counselling sequence which follows (deliberately like a marriage guidance counselling sequence) analyses what went wrong.

Showings and activities:

(1)   Show at least twice, without sound. Ask, *What happened?* Get the group to reconstruct the story-line: i.e. that Beckett was expecting a visitor, that a man came in, that Sandra assumed he was the visitor, etc. Once the group have reconstructed the story-line correctly, show the sequence again, still without sound.

If you have a small class (eight to ten students) we suggest dividing them into three or four groups and asking them to divide up the sequence into four mini-sequences; then have each group write a dialogue for its particular mini-sequence. These mini-sequences were chosen by one of the groups at Renault:

(a).   Sandra painting nails; Beckett speaks to her; man comes in; Sandra answers telephone while man waits; Sandra speaks to Beckett, then sends man into Beckett's office.

(b)   Beckett shakes man's hand; goes to ask Sandra for coffee; man on knees beside radiator; Beckett astonished.

(c)   Robbins arrives; begins to argue with Sandra, who has barred his way; Robbins storms out.

(d)   Man leaves Beckett's office; argument between Sandra and Beckett.

(*Note*: The groups were not asked to include everything in each mini-sequence – only those parts where it would be possible to write a dialogue.)

(2) Have each sub-group write and record (or improvise and record) the dialogues they have prepared. Correct and check the dialogues for content, mood, language intonation, etc. Check that the learners' dialogues hang together with the story-line and moods expressed in the video film by another showing without sound.

(3) Show video with sound. Before asking the normal comprehension questions, compare learners' dialogues with the script.

(4) Show again with sound. In this sequence, almost all the mistakes were Sandra's. Therefore we suggest getting learners to make a common list of her faults (not asking the visitor's name, etc.) before a showing to include the counselling sequence.

Further activities

(a) Role-playing on receiving visitors (politeness formulae, how to deal with rude visitors, how to make somebody wait, etc.).

(b) Discussion on how an organisation can improve its welcoming service for visitors. This is useful on in-company teaching programmes, as most companies have some weak link in the chain, e.g. parking facilities, reception desk communication, waiting areas, etc.

EXAMPLE 2

William the Silent (from *Manhunt*)
Sequences of a *Video Arts* management training film on interviewing techniques, also available on video.
Duration of sequence: approximately 10 minutes
Characters: William the Silent, an incompetent interviewer
Harding, a competent interviewer
The interviewee
Realia for activities: curriculum vitae, job description

Figures 16, 17   *Scenes from The Secretary and her Boss (featuring John Cleese, Adrienne Posta and Rosemary Leach)*

Story: the first sequence of the film deals with the problems of a shy man who has to interview a rather worldly young ex-public school man for a management position. The interviewer, though he may have his doubts about the interviewee's competence, is far too squeamish to ask potentially embarrassing questions. Thus the interviewee dominates throughout. The humour is mostly verbal. The second sequence follows immediately and shows the same interviewee with a competent interviewer.

Lesson plan: the teachers in the seminar judged this film to be extremely difficult on two levels − linguistic and cultural − and first reactions were fairly negative. The speed of the dialogue was criticised (as an interview situation is rarely visually obvious). Also the video was thought to be too British with its references to such things as *The Guardian*, A-levels, Harrow, etc. We therefore decided to show only the *William the Silent* part of the video, along with the correct interview by Harding, as these parts of the video were visually most comprehensible.

The lesson plan was as follows:

(1)   Show *William the Silent* and *Harding* sequences with sound.
(2)   Discuss, eliciting reactions; describing moods, social class, etc.
(3)   Show the first sequence only, stopping the video for vocabulary and comprehension. Practise asking questions based on the interviewee's comments; i.e. 'What questions should William have asked?'
(4)   Discuss attitudes of interviewee, situating his social background and competence.
(5)   Vocabulary exercise.
(6)   Show *William the Silent* and *Harding* sequences for the third time.
(7)   Curriculum vitae and job description activity.

Lesson: the lesson did not go as planned. Learners were divided as to whether William the Silent was an idiot, or a far more intelligent interviewer than Harding (on the theory that nobody as stupid as William could hold a management position − and he was therefore only pretending incompetence). This led to an animated discussion on interviewing techniques, with the teacher's interventions limited to correction.

After the discussion, the teacher tried to get learners to form the questions that the interviewer should have asked, but they were quickly bored by this activity (which involved stopping the video every few seconds) and were also rather disorientated by the necessarily directive attitude — at this stage — of the teacher.

A list of difficult phrases and sentences was then given out and checked over before a third showing of the film.

Learners were then divided into groups to study a curriculum vitae and job description, to prepare their questions for a mock interview. Each group then asked its questions, with the teacher as the interviewee. The activity seemed to work better. A vocabulary exercise was given out as homework and corrected the following morning.

Feedback: although the feedback was generally positive, several learners criticised what they saw as the insularity of *Manhunt*.

Figure 18   *John Cleese in Manhunt*

EXAMPLE 3

Where the houses used to be
A 50 minute documentary film about new high-rise housing developments in the East End of London, from Thames Television, also available on video.

Story: this documentary consists mainly of interviews with tenants on a new housing estate. The theme of the film underlines how, with the best intentions, town planners can make very bad mistakes by destroying 'slum' back-to-back houses and replacing them with blocks of flats. This documentary gives a very good insight into the attitudes of a close-knit London community when faced with the red tape of the town planners and local authorities. Most of the people in this film speak with strong Cockney accents.

Lesson plan: during the seminar the teachers watched the complete film and although some of the teachers found the language difficult to understand they decided that certain themes of the film could be exploited, as they presented common Anglo-French political problems (e.g. loneliness, vandalism, the destruction of traditional lifestyles, etc.). They then chose the parts of the film which were easier to understand, and which dealt with these themes. Five sequences were chosen.

Most of the teachers and learners found *Where the houses used to be* very moving.

The lesson was planned as follows:

(1) Show sequences 1–4 (about 20 minutes).
(2) Discuss, eliciting learners' reactions globally, then sequence by sequence.
(3) Show sequences 1–4 again, stopping the tape to check for global understanding. Explain key words, i.e. council flat, landing, kids, vandalism, etc.
(4) More general discussion about living in flats; comparing the situation in France to that in England.
(5) Show sequence 5 (the tenants' meeting).
(6) Discuss for global understanding.
(7) Show sequence 5 again.

(8) Role-play a tenants' meeting (using the following roles: local authority spokesman, police, tenants, social worker, landlord, etc.).

Lesson and feedback: unfortunately we had no detailed feedback, as the lesson was not completed for reasons of time. Nevertheless, learners seemed to enjoy both film and lesson.

4 CONCLUSION

As the situation regarding authentic video material is very much in flux as regards material available and technological and pedagogical expertise, perhaps we should confine ourselves to one short and fairly obvious conclusion.

Authentic video materials, if chosen and exploited with care, can play an important part in modern English language teaching. However, used without due thought or preparation, they can become an expensive waste of time for both teachers and learners.

9 *Exploiting Television Videos with Particular Reference to Teaching ESP*

SUSAN SHEERIN

Susan Sheerin has taught English as a foreign language and other modern languages in Canada and Germany as well as the UK. She is now a teacher and teacher trainer at the Colchester English Study Centre.

1 WHY A VIDEO?

Because expensive technological hard and software are not the universal panacea they are sometimes made out to be (one thinks of language laboratories as a case in point), it is a useful exercise to clarify our aims and objectives when using a video. It seems to me that there are at least four good reasons for using a television video in the classroom.

First, there is the obvious but nevertheless very important factor of added interest provided by a visual stimulus. The added interest increases learner motivation − always an important consideration − and, generally speaking, the video-tape has a great advantage over the audio-tape in this respect.

A second good reason for using a video is the opportunity it provides for learners to hear authentic language used in context. This is particularly relevant when teaching ESP: it is one way of presenting a particular variety of English as it is actually used by the group concerned, be it a talk by a consultant specialist on how family doctors can deal more effectively with liver disease or a discussion amongst engineers of some of the problems of metal fatigue. Usually the foreign learner studying in Britain is constantly exposed to normal everyday English, but if he is studying for occupational purposes, the spoken variety to do with his particular interest is much less accessible. Clearly audio-tapes may be found to help here but in many situations, such as demonstrations or discussions, the visual aspect is indispensable.

The third and most significant reason for using a video is to provide practice in listening comprehension. Here again, the visual aspect facilitates comprehension; it is a much more realistic exercise to try and understand the discourse of people you can actually see talking. When you teach listening comprehension, it is helpful to think of two levels — extensive listening and intensive listening.

The first level involves using a video purely to provide practice in listening and understanding. In this case, although the learner may not understand every word we want to train him to follow the main theme and recognise the most important points. This is called extensive listening, and the activities involved in this should be designed to encourage learners to listen for the general gist of a programme. This level of listening practice can be used quite successfully with intermediate learners of English as well as with the more advanced. It is also equally useful in the teaching of general English and ESP.

The second level, however, is for the more advanced learner and is probably most relevant in the teaching of ESP. It involves listening for specific words and/or phrases with a view to eventual production. This is the intensive listening phase and tasks for the learner should be aimed at making him isolate, identify, and produce certain items of language.

In the course of these activities the video will be used not only to consolidate material already known or half known, but also to present new ESP material in context. It is generally accepted by language teachers that the learner should hear and produce a new item of language before he reads it. This can present quite a problem when dealing with ESP material, and a video provides one way of dispensing with the rather uninteresting text crammed with unfamiliar specialist language which is often used as a vehicle for presentation in ESP courses.

In the teaching of general English, a television video is not an ideal way of presenting new structural items for low-level learners. One may find a particular video which uses a structure or function very frequently, but in a normal video the language is too uncontrolled for general English purposes. In the ESP situation, however, the portion of language we are interested in is limited and is therefore more manageable.

In the practice phase of the general English class, although an example of, say, the *past continuous interrupted*, which is heard somewhere on the tape, may be highly illustrative, this structure is not likely to occur very often. It seems rather arbitrary, then, to isolate this or any item for special attention and practice if it is only heard once or twice in a video that will probably be at least 20 minutes long. However, specialist words and phrases are liable to occur with sufficient frequency in the specialist tape to make their repeated practice a natural occurrence in any follow-up work.

The fourth and final reason for using a video is that it effectively stimulates further activity. Videos on social or political problems can be the start of a lively discussion or debate, which would be as useful in the general English as in the ESP situation.

2   WHERE TO START

For the sake of convenience the teacher needs to have something down on paper in order to analyse the video and plan extension work for it. If the programme or the extract one wishes to use is not too long it may be possible to make a transcript. However, this is a very laborious and time-consuming task and there are easier ways to solve the problem.

The first thing the teacher can do is to check the relevant back copy of the BBC's weekly magazine, *The Listener* (the week following the first transmission of the programme), in a reference library to see whether a summary and partial transcript has been printed. Failing this, the teacher can made a detailed summary using the counter on the video machine for ease of reference. The three videos I shall be using for exemplification in this article are *The Transplanted Self* (Part 1), *Try a Little Tenderness* and *The Keys to Paradise*[1], all of which can be used very usefully for listening practice with foreign doctors. The first two of these videos have indeed been printed in *The Listener*, but a teacher's summary had to be made for *The Keys to Paradise* of which the following is an extract:

085   There are two forms of morphine molecule like a key and its mirror image: one is a powerful drug; one is completely inactive, suggested Goldstein's first clue.

090   Goldstein elaborates − drug is inert, therefore there must be receptors in brain cells and they must be shaped to accommodate morphine molecule just as a lock accommodates a particular key.

098   Left-handed molecule acts upon the nerve cell. There should be a corresponding keyhole or receptor cell, but where?

103   If we follow one nerve fibre to another nerve cell it connects at terminals. At adjoining terminal (synapses), where cells exchange chemical messages, receptors or keyholes should be found. Difficult job − like finding a keyhole in a city.

113   Upsala University had techniques for research. Lars Terenius had been looking for steroid receptors. Logical progression to look for opium receptors. Used rats, brain homogenised (thin soup of cells), spun in centrifuge so cells from synapse area extracted.

After all the work on listening has been completed, the students should receive a transcript or a summary in order to reinforce what they have learned and to enable them to read it through and raise any remaining problems. If there is no transcript available the teacher's notes can be summarised, so that all the main points are included without too much extraneous detail, and given to the students.

3   EXPLOITATION

THE EXTENSIVE LISTENING PHASE

As already stated, the extensive listening lesson has the sole aim of teaching and practising the skill of listening with understanding.

There is no aim for the learner to practise or produce what he hears. The ability to understand any message is partly dependent on the ability to contextualise and anticipate the message. Because of this it is always a good idea to begin a listening comprehension lesson with a summary of what the learners are going to hear; and the less advanced the students are, the more detailed the summary needs to be. As this is strictly an exercise in listening, learners should need to use only the minimum of language in order to prove their understanding. Comprehension checks, such as questions requiring short answers, multiple choice questions, or questions requiring non-verbal responses (e.g. drawing a diagram) would thus be particularly appropriate. The important thing here is that the main points have been understood. The questions should reflect this and not be concerned with incidentals.

THE INTENSIVE LISTENING PHASE

Learners can be prepared for intensive listening with an extensive listening phase. One can, however, start straight in with intensive listening, depending on the level of the learners and the time available. The aim of an intensive listening lesson is to focus on particular specialist items of language and to enable the learners to use these. The tasks for the learners should reflect this aim and are most conveniently organised into some kind of worksheet which can be distributed before the first viewing (in this phase) of the video.

Each video has its own character and lends itself to particular activities. However, in trying to decide on the best way to exploit a video it may be helpful to think in terms of the following general areas.

VERBALISING VISUAL INFORMATION

Diagrams
Diagrams, graphs, histograms, etc. within the video can be reproduced and learners asked to explain or verbalise them. In videos where there are no such devices it will usually be possible to

arrange some of the information in diagrammatic form. For example, in *The Transplanted Self*, the information contained in the video is summarised at the end as follows:

> So a simple, but revealing, picture of the functioning human immune system was now beginning to fall into place. It was the culmination of the work of not one, but several, groups of scientists. There appeared to be two arms to the system, each depending on a different set of lymphocytes: one, the T-cell system, was under the control of the thymus; the other, the B-cell system, was under the control of whatever the equivalent of the bursa is in man.
>
> The place of origin of both the T-cells and the B-cells is the bone marrow. Cells known as stem cells pass from the bone marrow to the thymus where they become T-cells; or, alternatively, they become B-cells, which in turn can produce anti-bodies. Just as it happens that some children are born without a functioning B-cell system, and some are born without a functioning T-cell system, some are born without either. The condition is known as Severe Combined Immune Deficiency – SCID.

This information can be diagrammatised as in Figure 19.

Behaviour and Actions
One can use the simple but effective expedient of asking the learner to give a commentary on some part of the video with the sound turned down. This practises many skills. There are also other ways of exploiting the visual quality of a video. In *Try a Little Tenderness* Jonathan Miller demonstrates how patients' actions can tell doctors a lot about the nature of their complaint:

> If someone has a pain which is due to poor circulation through the muscles of the heart, he often presses the front of his chest with a clenched fist. The fact that he uses the whole fist indicates that the pain is pretty widespread, but because the hand is clenched at the same time, it also tells us that the pain has a gripping quality as if the chest was being crushed in a vice.

THE HUMAN IMMUNE SYSTEM AND 'SCID'

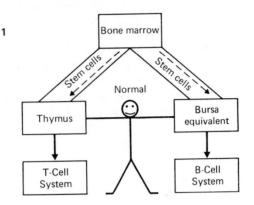

1

Bone marrow

Stem cells   Stem cells

Normal

Thymus   Bursa equivalent

T-Cell System   B-Cell System

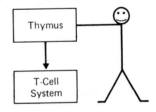

2a   **Immune Deficient**

Bursa equivalent

B-Cell System

2b   **Immune Deficient**

Thymus

T-Cell System

3   **Severe Combined Immune Deficiency (SCID)**

Explain the diagrams

Figure 19   *The Human Immune System and 'SCID'*

He goes on to examine other pointing gestures in a similar way, which can be used on a worksheet (see Exercise 1).

EXERCISE 1

Your teacher will now indicate pain in the same way as Jonathan Miller does in the film. Write down what each action suggests to you.

a) _____

b) _____

c) _____

d) _____

A similar procedure can be followed with any video containing some sort of demonstration which can practically be reproduced in the classroom.

IDENTIFYING CONNECTIONS AND RELATIONSHIPS

It is a very useful and indeed demanding exercise to ask learners to explain various connections. One can do this by looking at the video as a whole and, for example, asking the learner to say how the information is organised. This is an activity that gets right to the very heart of comprehension and is a very useful preparation for groups of, for example, study fellows who are going to have to attend, understand, and take useful notes from lectures.

One can also look at connections in microcosm, as it were, and the *Try a Little Tenderness* video, which is littered with colourful similes, lends itself nicely to the task shown in Exercise 2.

EXERCISE 2

Explain the connections between the following:

(a)	diagnosis of disease	and a jigsaw
(b)	the intestine	and an escalator
(c)	intestinal environment	and Florida
(d)	swallowing	and crossing the Rubicon
(e)	an oyster	and a villain
(f)	the appendix	and four or five o'clock
(g)	internal pain	and a stick in a glass of water

Even without such exuberant language, however, there should be ample opportunity for asking the learner to clarify points in this way. For example, the learner can be given the following information:

> In 1863 John Hilton published a book entitled *On Rest and Pain*, in which he argued that, whenever an organ or part was inflamed or irritated, the surrounding muscles went into a state of rigid spasm which immobilised the affected region. If a joint like the knee or the hip becomes affected or inflamed, the muscles which are normally responsible for moving the joint become unusually rigid and hold the joint still. This allows the injured part to rest, and . . . rest is an essential condition for repair and recovery.

He can then be asked to explain the relationship between inflammation and muscular rigidity.

REORGANISING INFORMATION

The teacher can always consider whether the information contained in a video might possibly be reorganised or regrouped in some way.

All three videos lend themselves well to this activity. For example, in *Try a Little Tenderness* the learners can be asked to fill in a case report form on the patient with appendicitis, rearranging the information given about him under the headings: Personal Details, Family History, Presenting Symptoms, Personal History, Review of Systems, Clinical Examination, Past Medical History, and Results of Investigations. Later, one of the class can present the case to his colleagues using only the form he has completed.

The Keys to Paradise and *The Transplanted Self* both follow the development of a particular area of research and this information can be reorganised as in the example of a worksheet for *The Keys to Paradise* (see Exercise 3).

Scientists	Place of Study	Area of Research	Experiments	Results	Implications
Avon Goldstein					
Lars Terenius			1.		
			2.		
Candice Pert			1.		
Huda Akil			2.		
David Mayer					
Hughes & Costerlitz					
Howard Morris					
Barry Morgan					

FOCUSING ON SPECIALIST VOCABULARY

It is a good idea to use cloze exercises or blank-filling exercises to focus on particular vocabulary. In the case of the doctors watching the *Try a Little Tenderness* video, one of the big problems for them is adjusting their language from doctor/patient to doctor/doctor language and vice versa. As Jonathan Miller conveniently uses both medical and lay terminology throughout his programme, the learners are given the following task:

EXERCISE 4
Fill in the blanks:

Doctor/patient language	*Doctor/doctor language*
1	gastralgia
2 stone in the kidney	
3 groin	
4 shingles	
5	abdomen
6 gut	
7	mucosa
8 colic	
9	diarrhoea
10	vomiting
11 gastro-enteritis	

Also, if the students are to be given a summary because no transcript is available, the crucial vocabulary to which the students' attention is being drawn can be clozed out.

4   FURTHER ACTIVITIES

While one should bear in mind the danger of over-exploiting any one video, there are nevertheless some activities which can follow on very naturally and usefully from a video. One of the films in the BBC *Engineering Craft Studies* series comes to mind, namely the one entitled *The Process of Production*.

This shows part of a very interesting board meeting, thus setting the situation and providing the personalities for a role-playing follow-up board meeting.

One can also ask the learner to relate the information in the video to his own situation in some way. If *The Keys to Paradise* were being shown, learners could be asked to give an account of some research project with which they have been involved or to give evidence based on their practical experience of the variation of pain thresholds among patients. Following *The Transplanted Self*, learners can describe the present state of immunological research in their own countries.

Finally there is the discussion or debate which must perforce follow any video of a controversial or sensational character. Doctors and patients alike inevitably find they have something to say on the subject of the relationship between hospital doctors and patients when they see *Try a Little Tenderness*. This is only natural and should not be suppressed but welcomed as the final free phase in production.

In conclusion, the use of television videos can prove very valuable on ESP courses. Many interesting factual programmes like those in the *Horizon*, *The Body in Question* and *Engineering Craft Studies* series already mentioned can be hired or bought from BBC Publications Enterprises Ltd. In making use of this wealth of excellent material in an imaginative way, the ESP teacher can be sure of giving a lesson that is both interesting and highly relevant to the needs of the learners.

NOTES

[1] *The Transplanted Self* (Part 1), Film & Video Catalogue Supplement no. 616.4 (BBC Enterprises Ltd, 1980).
Try a Little Tenderness from *The Body in Question*, Film & Video Catalogue Supplement no. 612 (BBC Enterprises Ltd, 1980).
The Keys to Paradise from *Horizon*, Film & Video Supplement no. 612.8 (BBC Enterprises Ltd, 1980).

10 *The Self-Instruction Video Module – A Solution in ESP*

VALERIE BEVAN

Valerie Bevan taught English as a foreign language in the UK before going to work in Germany. She has taught and designed materials for ESP and advanced general English courses at the British Council's centre in Munich and at the Free University of Berlin, where she is now working on a research project.

The module for the film *The House and the Sun*[1](see pp146–53)was written to help students who came to the British Council centre in Munich from the Chief Planning and Building Authority in the Bavarian State Ministry of the Interior. These students were specialists from three different areas: road and bridge construction, water management, and architecture. They had a common goal in that they all wanted to improve their ability to communicate, mainly orally, with English-speaking fellow specialists visiting Bavaria. They all needed training in social skills; in discussion skills as appropriate to informal situations, small group meetings and conferences; in explaining the functions and organisation of the Authority and their own roles within it; and in giving and understanding oral exposition of technical points both at specialist level in their own particular areas of interest, and more generally in connection with major projects undertaken by the Authority in other areas.

As far as the technical aspects of these needs were concerned, up to a certain point students were interested in one another's work and prepared to consult one another when the matter under discussion was outside their own specialism. Thereafter their knowledge, interests and lexical needs diverged widely. Two series of exercises were accordingly produced for each specialist area to present and practise some of the technical English the students needed.

1 A series of progressively difficult teacher-directed classroom and language laboratory exercises which were done by the whole class. In pair or small group exercises, non-specialists and specialists were put together and the specialists were given tasks that required them to fulfil consultant roles.

2 A series of exercises designed for self-instruction based on a videofilm dealing with a topic in the specialist area: the self-instruction video module. This was constructed as follows.

   Each section of the film was supported by a pre-viewing exercise intended to supply the more difficult vocabulary in a form which would make students engage with it, either by means of a straightforward language exercise or by posing a technical problem, the discussion and solution of which would involve the terms to be learnt (from other students or a specialist dictionary) and to be practised. (Like many other students of ESP who are practising professionals with their school study of English many years behind them, these students had concentrated on the written word when they last learnt English, and felt more confident if new vocabulary was seen before it was heard. Those who occasionally read professional literature in English would often recognise technical terms on the printed page, but not when heard – unless they were expecting them.)

   The pre-viewing exercise was followed by an instruction to watch the particular section of film which answered the question, checked the exercise, or provided a solution to the problem presented at the pre-viewing phase. This section of film was identified by the video counter numbers as a way of locating the section when the students wanted to repeat it, and by the last words of commentary heard in that section.

   There might then be a post-viewing exercise, intended to consolidate and extend the language acquired and practised in the previous two phases.

When the first series of teacher-directed exercises had been completed for all three specialist areas, the students were shown how to operate the video player and monitor. Members of each specialist group were given their respective worksheets for a self-instruction video module and the corresponding video film to work with independently. The teacher went from group to group to deal with any difficulties that might arise − either such linguistic ones that could not be resolved within the group, even with the aid of a suitable dictionary, or those that derived from the formulation of the question. In this case the teacher consulted the students so that the exercise could be corrected or made clearer in subsequent versions of the worksheet.

Each module took between 4 and 5 hours and was done over three or four class meetings, at which other kinds of exercises concerned with different needs were also done. On each occasion, one of the three groups was recorded at work, simply by focusing the video camera on the group as they seated themselves in front of the video set, and leaving it running. This recording was later seen by the teacher, and selected excerpts from it were used at the next class meeting, not only for remedial work, but to draw attention to instances of particularly effective language use. This procedure was both instructive, in that the students learnt from each other, and encouraging, in that they saw how much had already been learnt and was being learnt.

By recording one group at work the teacher was able to monitor it *in absentia* − and much more effectively, given the complexity of the text, the exercises and the students' interactions, than would have been possible with an audio tape recorder. Thus most of the teacher's time during the class session could be spent with the other two groups, without the third feeling that they were at a disadvantage. The recordings made of the students at work, however, revealed that they also had much to teach the designer about the effectiveness of the small group's use of the self-instruction video module, and how this was affected by the presence or absence of the teacher.

Students seemed to get used to the video camera quickly and forgot it, as they did not forget the presence of an observer who

Figure 20

was monitoring their use of language, and could be consulted in a linguistic crisis. In the teacher's absence they concentrated more fully on using English to achieve genuinely communicative ends, and experimentation usually took the form of the student trying a different construction or different lexis if he felt he had not made himself understood to his colleagues by his initial gambit. When the teacher was present, students became more (though by no means unconstructively) concerned with correctness, and would also experiment with new constructions and unfamiliar lexis to find out if 'that is how you say it in English'. That is to say, the camera was not a mere substitute for the teacher's eyes and ears, but actually provided significantly different, and equally valuable learning conditions.

At the same time, the camera revealed the wide range of language functions stimulated by the exercise structure. The following are some examples from transcripts of video recordings.

1 THE PRE-VIEWING PHASE

ORGANISING HOW AN EXERCISE IS DEALT WITH

1 *Group*: engineers specialising in road and bridge construction
   Topic: the construction of a London flyover
   Task: labelling a diagram of the flyover with the terms supplied
   A : But we . . . I think we should begin with the first term, and there's *dual carriageway road.*

B : Yes, it's a two lane . . . a two lane road. Let's go from the great things [*sic* — the more general terms] to the details.

Group: architects
Topic: solar energy and house design
Task: explaining the so-called *greenhouse effect* by means of a diagram.

(The group have decided to have one member draw the diagram, which is to be subject to their suggestions and criticism.)

A : (referring to the instructions, but modifying them slightly so that he is also addressing the architect standing at the flip chart beside the video set, ready to begin drawing)
And now, please, give a brief explanation of this effect, by using diagrams if you wish.

B : And now you have to . . .

C : Make a drawing, please.

The diagram-drawer: So you tell me what I shall draw, and I shall do it. I should explain the greenhouse.

B : You should make a cross-section . . .

The diagram-drawer: (beginning to draw) Make a cross-section . . .

B : Through a greenhouse.

The diagram-drawer: Through a greenhouse. And this greenhouse . . .

C : Is part of a house.

A : (reading) Is a room built onto the front, the back or the side of a house.

A difference of opinion in the course of doing an exercise
(The architect drawing the diagram has been explaining it as he proceeds.)

The diagram-drawer: And I think at night, you need curtains, something like this . . .

A : I don't quite agree with this construction (getting up) I think that it's important that you don't have a heavy wall at this point (pointing to the diagram) so that the heat can come through the house as far as it is possible.

2 THE VIEWING PHASE

OPERATING THE VIDEO SET

1 *The student operating the set*: (looking at the counter) It's on 196. Is that correct?
  Another student: *190*
  The operator: (pressing *rewind*) 190 . . . Right.
2 *The operator*: We can use the *pause* button if you want to discuss this.
  Another student: I would like to see the last part again.

NOTICING LEXIS, CHECKING PRONUNCIATION

(This response to the video film, exemplifed here by the architects, was common to all three groups.)

Film commentary: In Britain, conventional houses should have small windows to conserve heat, unless these windows are orientated to make use of solar energy. There is a well-known example which makes use of the sun to heat the space. The temperature inside the conservatory will be above
A : *space*
the outside temperature, even on light cloudy days. This is due to a
B : *cloudy* days
property of glass producing what is called the *greenhouse effect*. Shortwave radiation from the sun is able to pass through glass.
C : *radiation from the sun*

CORRECTING THE PRE-VIEWING EXERCISE

Group: engineers specialising in water management

Film commentary: These two functions, of screen and macerator, can be combined in the comminutor, where as the drum rotates against fixed blades, the solid particles are shredded between hardened steel cutters. (Music)[2]

A :   The solid particles are *shredded*.

B :   (referring to the group's answer in the completion exercise) *Shredded*, not *destroyed*.

A :   No, *shredded*.

COMPARING A SOLUTION TO A PRE-VIEWING PROBLEM WITH THAT GIVEN IN THE FILM

Group: architects

The diagram-drawer: (pressing the *pause* button to hold the diagram in the film corresponding to his own on the flip chart, and getting up to point to similarities between the two) So I don't think I was so wrong as you told me. It's the same principle!

In doing the exercises the students propose, agree and disagree, confirm, make suggestions, give instructions, give (polite) orders, express opinions, make statements, and make requests. Their consultations are based on, and produce, written texts and diagrams by means of which new lexis is acquired and rehearsed. The pronunciation of this lexis is checked and the meaning usually confirmed by the videofilm, a section of which can of course be repeated as often as the students find necessary. Gesture is used as an integral part of the communication.

Such examples of student interaction make the advantages of students working on the self-instruction video module in groups of three to five so evident that they might distract attention from what would otherwise be obvious from a glance at the worksheet: that the structure is eminently suitable for individual self-access use. Indeed, most modules written for small groups require the minimum of adaptation to be turned to this purpose. Thus they become a resource to be used to cope with such contingencies as one stray specialist in a class whose interests are in other areas, or an outstanding student whose fellow specialists are not yet good enough at English to be able to tackle the module with him.

It is as well that this is so, since the preparation of a self-instruction video module is demanding, time-consuming work. The very advantage of using authentic film texts (the ESP teacher can bring the native-speaker specialist and the specialist's environment into the classroom) means that the text in itself is often a challenge to the layman, and the process of didacticising the material usually presents one with many more problems. An accurate transcript is of course indispensable, and making it may involve a lot of reference work. Further research is then required to check technicalities and find complementary reading texts and diagrams. Some diagrams may need to be reproduced from the film.

There are, however, certain immediate compensations for one's labour, as well as the possible long-term usefulness of the module. One is that you inevitably find yourself very much better informed at the end of writing the worksheet, and therefore better equipped to follow the students' discussions, and to assist with lexis and pronunciation. You are also better equipped not only to teach but to learn from your students something of their specialities – one of the pleasures of teaching ESP. In view of the evidence provided by the transcripts of recordings of the students at work on the video module, I think I need hardly say that another compensation is its efficacy, and students' satisfaction.

Technical note: the design of the self-instruction video module was facilitated by three features of the Sony 2030 U-matic videocassette player which are unfortunately not replicated by every type of videocassette player.

1　The precision and reliability of the counter, which made possible the easy location of a section of videofilm by the same player used on different occasions and by different players of the same type.

2　The fact that when the *stop* button is pressed there is no hiatus in the film on resumption of the *play* function.

3   The fact that, used in conjunction with KCA or KCS type videocassettes, it permits the holding of a still picture on the screen for up to several minutes without wearing out the tape or damaging the machine.

3   THE HOUSE AND THE SUN

This module, although written for a specialist group of architects, one of whom chose the film, has been used successfully in courses for advanced students from a variety of backgrounds. In these cases, the more technical pre-viewing exercises were tackled with a mixture of general knowledge and ingenuity. They were either referred to someone with technical interests who happened to be in the group, or not done at all at the pre-viewing phase, but used to focus attention on the theme of the corresponding section of film and done as a comprehension exercise when it had been viewed. The last solution is not recommended, and would not be necessary in the case of modules written with students of general English in mind, a purpose to which the structure is obviously just as well suited as to ESP.

The part of the commentary which was recorded onto a sound cassette for use at Step 17 is printed *italics* on the transcript.

TRANSCRIPT

The sun provides the earth with a steady source of energy 5,000 times greater than that required by each person in an industrialised country. The only use we make of this energy income is in the minute amount converted by plants into food and timber. We rely instead on our energy capital, the limited resources of coal, oil and gas. In the United Kingdom, these are consumed at a rate equivalent to 5 electric fires, kept continuously on, for every man, woman and child. Much fuel is wasted in generating electricity, but our homes consume 48% of all that is produced, and our whole standard of living is dependent on its availability.

The largest single demand for energy is for heating a home. This need alone consumes 20% of all fossil fuel used in the UK.

Three-quarters of the fuel used for heating is wasted, mainly through poor design and construction. Houses are seldom grouped in a way that will conserve heat, and trees or shrubs are never planted to screen houses from cold northerly winds. High insulation standards will improve comfort and help conserve heat, but this is just one factor. Others, such as the shape of the house, the size and orientation of windows and type of construction should all be carefully considered. Natural ventilation can account for over 15% of the heat wasted. If we were to seal all the windows and draught-strip doors, then by adding insulation to the roof-loft and cavity walls we could cut the fuel bill by as much as one-third. Ventilation air could be drawn from the roof-loft in controlled amounts by using a fan. This air would be pre-heated by the sun even during the winter months.

We continue to neglect many useful principles that were well understood by the people who built our old houses and villages. For example, the village form was compact enough to provide some protection from cold winds but the layout also allowed adequate sunlight to reach individual houses and gardens. The houses are also compact in shape, and this helped to conserve heat as well as materials. The main windows face south whenever possible, and those on the north side are smaller, or dispensed with altogether. The careful use of local building materials produced details that also contributed to fuel savings. Small windows help reduce heat losses, and walls and roofs were well insulated because of the type of material that was used. The north-facing roof of this 2-storey house in Sussex reaches nearly to the ground. Well-insulated, its shape was inspired by local traditional building. There are windows on the north side, but these are only narrow strips for looking out.

On the south side, the architect, Michael Cassidy, has made the wall entirely of glass, to take advantage of the views and to make use of free heat from the sun. Solar radiation passing through the glass is absorbed by the internal walls and quarry-tiled floor. Comfort in the house is achieved by radiant heat rather than high temperatures. The main radiation comes from the sun shining directly through the glass wall, and from solar heat in the floor and internal walls. When these free radiant sources are no longer effective, as on cloudy days and at night, an electric radiant ceiling is switched on. Heavy curtains insulate the rooms at night, and large opening windows allow cool ventilation during the summer.

In contrast to more northern climates, the houses of the Mediterranean region were constructed to keep the dwellings cool inside during the summer months. To exclude direct sunlight, the windows are small, but the most important feature of the houses is their thick walls of mud-block or stone. These heavy walls absorb the heat of the sun during the day, and prevent this heat from reaching the inside until the evening. The walls in effect iron out the extremes of day and night-time temperature. Light-coloured roofing tiles reflect much of the sun's radiation, and the closely-packed houses provide mutual shading, and cool streets.

A positive approach to the use of solar energy led architect Dominic Michaelis to give traditional methods a modern interpretation in this house in the south of France. A belt of pine trees shelters the house from the cold NW winds which often blow in this area. A departure from local tradition are the main windows, which are large to allow sunshine to warm the rooms during the cooler times of the day and year. But these are shaded from strong sunlight by recessing the glass to form balconies. The rest of the wall area is of local stone, and used in the traditional way to soak up the heat of the day and keep the interior cool. Solar heat penetrates to the rooms only during the early morning and evening, and through the south-facing windows during the winter. Like the Sussex house, the solar heat is stored in the heavy walls and floor and helps warm the interior. The rooms are arranged on split levels, which ascend in a spiral. The living rooms form a series of interconnecting spaces around a central core. This core contains all the piped services, and a store at the bottom of the core provides supplementary heating during the winter. Warm air circulates up through the living rooms and the staircase that connects the bedrooms above. The staircase finishes on a roof terrace.

In Britain, conventional houses should have small windows to conserve heat unless these windows are orientated to make use of solar energy. There is a well-known example which makes use of the sun to heat the space. The temperature inside the conservatory will be above outside temperature, even on light cloudy days. This is due to a property of glass producing what is called *the greenhouse effect*. Shortwave radiation from the sun is able to pass easily through glass. This warms up solid materials such as wall and floor. This re-radiates heat, but this is in the form of longwave radiation which cannot pass back through the glass, and causes the temperature to rise. Used in the right way, conservatories can help insulate living rooms against heat losses during the winter.

Built in 1961, this school on the exposed Wirral Peninsula presents to the north a very solid, well-insulated structure, but the designer, Emslie Morgan, used the greenhouse effect to heat the building, so that, from the south, the school looks like a large conservatory. The solar heat gained through the glass wall is stored in the concrete roof and floors, and in the solid walls. The high thermal mass of this brick and concrete envelope prevents excessive swings of internal temperature. Heat gained from occupants and lighting is also important. Fresh air ventilators are opened during the summer, but for most of the year ventilation is kept to a minimum to conserve heat. The glass wall is broken up by a pattern of ventilator windows to classrooms on two floors, and by solid panels which form the end walls of storage rooms. The solar wall consists of two skins of glass. The outer layer is clear, and the inner skin is obscure to reduce glare. A special vertical duct is provided at the ends of the solar wall to allow air in the space between the skins of glass to expand. The clear glass ventilators pivot open to allow outside air into the classrooms. And adjustable ventilator-shutters in the back wall of the school can be opened to produce through-ventilation. The pin-up boards in the classrooms also act as heat-absorbing panels. Well-insulated on the inside, the other side is faced with aluminium sheeting which is painted black to absorb solar energy during the winter. This helps heat the classroom. These sheets can be reversed so that solar radiation is reflected back from the polished side during the summer.

The other solid panels in the solar wall also absorb or reject solar heat. Made of brick, they are covered with white-painted wooden shutters to reflect radiation during the summer, but when solar heating is needed the shutters hinge open, and the black painted wall then absorbs the solar energy. This development of the conservatory idea could be applied to houses. Users would quickly learn how to adjust the various devices to achieve comfort throughout the year.

At the French solar laboratories, Professor Felix Trombe has been researching into the controlled use of the greenhouse effect for heating dwellings.

Whereas in the school the heat was stored in the heavy construction which surrounded the whole space, in this case the mass is concentrated in one wall. This wall consists of concrete with a sheet of glass placed in front of it. The construction is built into the south face of the house, and normal windows can be placed between these solely collecting walls. The wall collects solar energy from the low sun during the winter months. This temperature builds up, due to the greenhouse effect, and provides a source of heat for use during the evenings, at night, and on cloudy days. In principle the remainder of the house should be of lightweight construction, and well-insulated. Insulation is also needed behind the solar wall to conserve the stored heat. A shutter is placed at the top of the wall to control the direction of warm air. A shutter is also needed at the bottom to allow unheated air to circulate up the face of the wall. This shutter can be closed to stop cold air from entering the room when the wall is not hot enough to cause the air to circulate upwards. When heating is required the shutters are set to allow warm air to pass into the room at the top. This rising air is replaced by the cooler air through the bottom of the wall, and in this way a continuous circulation is achieved which transfers the stored heat from the wall to the room. By opening ventilators at the back of the room the wall now assists in cooling by natural ventilation. The houses incorporating the Trombe wall were designed by Jacques Michel, who is now applying the principle to multi-storey apartment blocks.

The examples we have seen so far have made use of the building itself as a solar energy collector. By careful design and choice of materials, simple principles have been applied to the selective use of the sun's energy to help with space heating. This passive approach is complemented by a developing solar technology aimed at harnessing the sun's energy by more direct means. For example, one method is to focus solar radiation to achieve higher temperatures. This is demonstrated in such simple devices as portable water heaters and solar cookers. The disadvantages of these are that they have to track with the sun and of course only work in direct sunlight.

This large focusing collector is at Odeillo in the French Pyrenees. Rows of mirrors on a hillside are focused onto a large parabolic mirror behind the solar furnace. This mirror in turn focuses the solar radiation onto a small area. Very high temperatures can be achieved, and it is conceivable that units like this could in the future be applied to generating electricity by means of steam turbines.

Another method for the future might be the use of solar cells to convert sunlight directly into electricity. The cells are at the moment very expensive and a large area would be needed to produce sufficient electricity to run a home. Most development work is being done on flat plate solar collectors. In the panels being tested here, water is used as the collecting medium. This circulates behind sheets of glass, and the heated water is then stored for use over a period of time.

This barn is typical of the many experimental installations of this type in Britain and on the Continent. The existing roof is covered with the lines of collector panels consisting of batches of polythene hose-piping. These will be covered with glass so that the greenhouse effect will concentrate the heat of the sun around the pipes. Circulating water is run through the collector, and the heated water will be piped to a storage tank until needed. In this case the hot water will circulate in pipes under the floor of this workshop, to provide low-temperature background heating.

Government-sponsored agencies are showing a growing interest in the use of flat plate collectors. Two housing schemes, by the French electricity authority, have solar collecting panels built into the homes. A group of five houses at Le Havre in Northern France will incorporate inclined panels on the roof. Their efficiency will be compared with a similar group of houses at Aramand in the south of France.

Here the collectors are arranged vertically, and face south and south-west. The vertical panels collect solar heat from the winter sun to help with space heating. At Le Havre, spring and autumn heating is also needed, so the panels are inclined at an angle, to collect solar energy over a longer period of time. By using the solar heated water as a supplement to the usual electric hot-water and space heating system, savings of up to 70% on the annual fuel bill are expected to be made.

In Milton Keynes New Town, the development corporation, with the aid of a government grant, has converted a standard terrace house to solar space and water heating. The system was completed in March 1975, and is based on research done at the Polytechnic of Central London. The bedrooms and kitchen are arranged on two floors at the north side of the house, with a double-height living-room across the front, facing south. The lightweight construction, incorporating large, north-facing windows and normal insulation, is not ideal for solar heating, but it will allow fuel savings for this house to be compared with fuel costs for a similar house not using solar energy. The solar-collecting panels rest on the south-facing roof rafters. Made of aluminium, the panels are painted matt-black to increase the amount of solar energy absorbed. The whole collector is covered with glass. Water is circulated through the panel and into the top of a large hotwater storage tank. This tank is connected to a similar one on the floor below, and together they are calculated to hold enough solar-heated water for two days' heating for the typical autumn and spring needs. Heating is done by a warm-air blower under the stairs, and water from the storage tank is piped to the heater as required. The circuits are self-regulating and run by two pumps. When the temperature of the water drops below pre-set levels, a gas-fired boiler switches on automatically to boost the temperature. To make the best use of solar energy in this way, the house should be designed to minimise heat losses. Although this house is of low thermal efficiency, savings on the heating bill are expected to be over half of those for an unconverted house.

Solar collectors form part of the south wall of this experimental house, built in 1972 by a group called Street Farmers. The idea developed out of a concern for our dependence on diminishing material and energy resources, and on the environmental pollution caused in exploiting these. Careful design and the use of materials are combined with wind, rain, sun and biological cycles to find out how self-sufficient a home could become. One of the main factors that shaped the house was the need to cut out traditional fuels· altogether. The sleeping and winter living rooms are contained at first floor level in a very well insulated structure. The windows from these rooms look down into the greenhouse and so heat losses are cooking and nutrients for feeding plants. Rain water is collected, filtered, and purified for use. The greenhouse became more than a place to grow food out of season: it is made the natural extension of the living area, and also helps keep the rest of the house warm during the winter.

The *Street Farm* house is unique, but the principles represented by it and in the other examples we have seen are universal. By applying these principles with care, the sun can help save us fuel. But will we design or modify our homes to make these savings possible?

STUDENT WORKSHEET

THE HOUSE AND THE SUN

Work through the steps *in sequence*.

Step 1   Pre-question
The following figures are missing from the introduction to the film, reproduced below:

$$48\%   \quad 5 \quad   20\% \quad ¾ \quad 5,000$$

Put them in the appropriate gaps. You may discuss your conclusions with your colleagues.

The sun provides the earth with a steady source of energy
times greater than that required by each person in an industrialised
country. The only use we make of this energy income is in the

minute amount converted by plants into food and timber. We rely instead on our energy capital, the limited resources of coal, oil and gas. In the United Kingdom, these are consumed at a rate equivalent to   electric fires, kept continuously on, for every man, woman and child. Much fuel is wasted in generating electricity, but our homes consume   of all that produced and our whole standard of living is dependent on its availability.

The largest single demand for energy is for heating a home. This need alone consumes   of all fossil fuel used in the UK.   of the fuel used for heating is wasted, mainly through poor design and construction.

Step 2   Viewing (video counter nos. 000–052 '. . . through poor design and construction.')
Now check your version of the commentary against the original.

You may replay the section as often as you need to, but do not go beyond the last number on the video counter. The last words spoken are quoted after the second number.

Step 3   Pre-viewing exercise
Make a quick list of six electrical appliances that might be used in a typical West European household early in the morning, before work and school begin.

Step 4   Viewing (video counter nos. *023*–048. No commentary).
Compare your list with those appliances pictured in the film, adding any which you did not think of.

Step 5   Pre-viewing discussion exercise
What factors account for the high wastage of fuel used in heating?

Discuss this question briefly with your colleagues, and make brief notes of your group's main points.

Step 6   Viewing (video counter nos. 048–104 '. . . because of the type of material that was used')
Now make notes, under the headings given below, of the factors mentioned in the film.

Design

Materials

Location of houses in relation to each other

Step 7 *Viewing exercise* (video counter nos. 104–140)

Stage 1 Find the *Volume control* on the video monitor and reduce the volume to zero.

You will now be able to watch the next section of film without the sound.

As you do so, discuss the features of this architect-designed house – a house inspired by local traditional building – which help to minimise heat loss and take advantage of free heat from the sun. Make notes or sketches of these features.

Remember that you can play a section of film more than once, and that you can use the *pause* button.

Stage 2 (video counter nos. 104–140 '. . . cool ventilation during the summer.')

Now rewind the videofilm to the beginning of the section, return the volume control to its normal position and play the commentary, adding to your notes any expressions (such as *quarry-tiled floor*) which are new and may be useful to you.

Step 8 *Pre-viewing discussion question*
How does the design of traditional Mediterranean village houses regulate temperature?

Discuss this question briefly with your colleagues, making notes of your group's main points.

Step 9 *Viewing exercise* (video counter nos. 140–160 '. . . and cool streets.')
Compare your ideas with those in the film, adding any details your group omitted.

Step 10   Pre-viewing exercise
Complete the following section of commentary. All of the missing words are verb forms.

A positive approach to the use of solar energy   architect Dominic Michaelis to give traditional methods a modern inter-pretation in this house in the south of France. A belt of pine trees   the house from the cold NW winds which often   in this area. A departure from local tradition are the main windows, which are large to allow sunshine to   the rooms during the cooler times of the day and year. But these are   from strong sunlight by recessing the glass to form balconies. The rest of the wall area is of local stone, and used in the traditional way to   the heat of the day and keep the interior cool. Solar heat   to the rooms only during the early morning and evening, and through the south facing windows during the winter. Like the Sussex house, this solar heat is   in the heavy walls and floor and helps warm the interior. The rooms are   on split levels, which   in a spiral. The living rooms   a series of inter-connecting spaces around a central core. This core   all the piped services, and a store at the bottom of the core   supplementary heating during the winter. Warm air   up through the living rooms and the staircase that   the bedrooms above. The staircase finishes on a roof terrace.

Step 11   Viewing (video counter nos. 160–206 '. . . finishes on a roof terrace.')
Compare your version with the original. Where there are differences, discuss these with your colleagues or, if necessary, consult a dictionary to check the appropriateness of your version. Your teacher may also be consulted.

Step 12   Pre-viewing exercise
A *conservatory* is a building or a room built onto the front, back or side of a house, with glass walls and roof, in which plants are protected from the cold. The warmth of this room is due to a property of glass which produces what is called the *greenhouse effect*. Give a brief explanation of this effect, using diagrams if you wish.

Step 13 Viewing (video counter nos. 206–228 '. . . against heat losses during the winter.')
Make notes of any expressions that could have made your explanation clearer.

Step 14 Pre-viewing exercise
Complete the following section of tapescript using your own phrases.

Built in 1961, this school on the exposed Wirral Peninsula presents to the north a very solid, well-insulated structure, but the designer, Anthony Morgan, used the '   ' to heat the building, so that from the south, the school looks like a large conservatory.
                    gained through the glass wall is stored in the concrete roof and floors and in the solid walls. The high thermal mass of this brick and concrete envelope prevents excessive
            Heat gained from   is also important. Fresh air ventilators are opened   , but for most of the year, ventilation is kept to a minimum   . The glass wall is broken up by a pattern of ventilator windows to classrooms on two floors, and by solid panels which form the end walls of storage rooms. The solar wall consists of two skins of glass. The outer layer is clear, and the inner skin   to reduce glare. A special vertical duct is provided at the ends of the solar wall to allow air in the space between the skins of glass to expand. The clear glass ventilators pivot open to allow outside air into the classrooms. And adjustable ventilator-shutters in the back wall of the school can be opened to produce through-ventilation. The pin-up boards in the classrooms also act as heat-absorbing panels. Well-insulated on the inside, the other side is faced with aluminium sheeting which is painted   solar energy during the winter. This helps heat the classroom. These sheets can be reversed so that solar radiation   from the polished side during the summer.
    The other solid panels in the solar wall also absorb or reject solar heat. Made of brick, they are covered with   wooden shutters to reflect radiation during the summer but when solar

heating is needed the shutters hinge open, and the black painted wall then absorbs the solar energy. This development of the conservatory idea could be applied to houses. Users would quickly learn   the various devices to achieve comfort throughout the year.

Step 15   Viewing (video counter nos. 228–280 '. . . comfort throughout the year.')
Compare your version with the original. Where there are differences, do not assume that you are wrong. On the contrary. This exercise allows many possible correct answers. Your suggestions may be discussed with your colleagues, or you may consult the teacher.

Step 16   Post-viewing discussion exercise
What do you think of the design of the school on the Wirral Peninsula? Make brief notes of your group's conclusions.

Step 17   Pre-viewing exercise
Listen to the audio cassette, and choose a member of your group to make a sketch diagram of Professor Trombe's use of the greenhouse effect for heating dwellings. The group should give the drawer of the diagram all the assistance they can. You may, of course, stop the cassette and/or repeat sections as often as you like.

Step 18   Viewing (video counter nos. 280–328 '. . . to multi-storey apartment blocks.')
Compare your group's diagram with those given in the film. Where there are differences, are these mistakes?

Step 19   Pre-viewing exercise
In consultation with your colleagues, list uses of solar energy other than for space heating.

Step 20   Viewing exercise (video counter nos. 328–352 '. . . by means of steam turbines.')
List any uses of solar energy shown in this part of the film that your group did not think of.

Step 21   Post-viewing exercise

In 1882 *De Natuur* carried a report of a printing press (Figure 21) driven by solar energy which had been demonstrated by Abel Pifre, an engineer, in Paris. Water, heated in a cylinder in the centre of a concave reflector by the rays of the sun, produced steam, and the energy so obtained was used to power the printing press.

What did this invention have in common with a) the solar cooker; b) the focusing collector at Odeillo shown in the part of the film you have just seen?

Step 22   Viewing: Flat Plate Solar Collectors (video counter nos. 352–389 '. . . on the annual fuel bill are expected to be made.')

The illustration and diagrams in Figure 22 from *Solar Energy, A do-it-Yourself Manual* by Charles Kiely (Hamlyn, 1977, pp 31–2) will help you to understand this part of the film. Look at them before you watch the film.

Step 23   Post-viewing exercise

The film *The House and the Sun* was made in 1974. Since then, in Germany at least, optimism about the usefulness of flat plate solar collectors has not always been justified by experimental installations. In April 1980, the *Frankfurter Rundschau* published the following article. Read it with the aim of finding out how the solar collectors installed by Energieversorgung Schwaben have proved unsatisfactory.

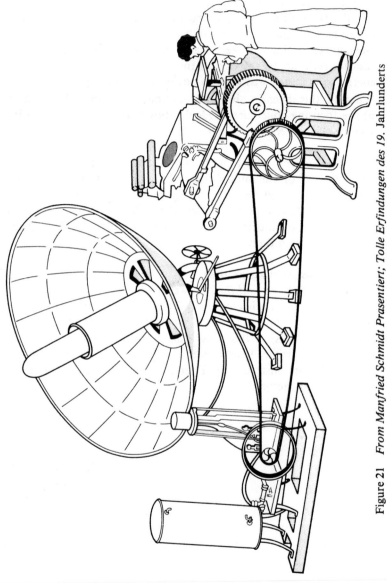

Figure 21 *From Manfried Schmidt Prasentiert; Tolle Erfindungen des 19. Jahrlunderts*

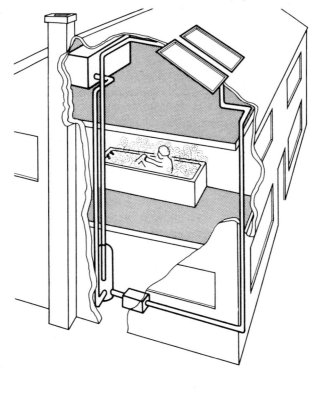

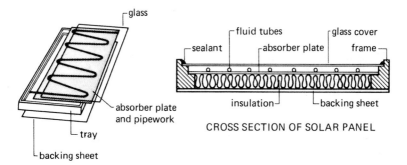

CROSS SECTION OF SOLAR PANEL

Figure 22

TRIAL CHANGES IN SOLAR HEAT TECHNIQUE

More and more experts seem to be arriving at the conclusion that solar collectors are outdated. Brown, Bowri & Cie of Mannheim announced last year that they were converting their experimental domestic solar collectors into heat absorbers combined with a heat pump.

Bosch-Junkers now report that they too have converted their tritherm experimental home. Solar collectors on the roof have been replaced by two different absorber systems, one based on copper, the other on steel.

Both say conversion was made necessary by the unsatisfactory performance of solar collectors. In 1977/78 solar collectors on the roof of the tritherm house met only 19 per cent of a well-insulated building's heating requirements.

Energieversorgung Schwaben, the power utility, has reported disappointment with the solar collectors on its solar-powered experimental home in Wangen.

'If you opt for central heating powered by solar collectors,' the company's house journal comments, 'you have backed the wrong horse. And so for water heating, they still need considerable improvement.'

Solar collectors are matt-finish black surfaces that collect heat from sunlight. Water runs through tubes in the black and taps the heat. The absorbent surface is glass-clad to prevent radiation of heat back into the environment.

Absorbers are also sheets mainly dark in colour that are criss-crossed inside with cooler tubes. These tubes are attached to the cold side of a heat pump, so they ensure the sheets are always a few degrees colder than their surroundings.

But because absorber sheet surfaces, unlike those of solar collectors, come into direct contact with the surrounding air they are also able to absorb heat from air and rain.

Even wind that whistles across the surface of absorber sheets thus supplies energy, whereas the glass cladding of solar collectors insulates them from the environment.

Solar collectors can unquestionably produce warm water, and

hot water even in good sunlight. But too little heat gets to where it is needed, according to the power utility.

At their experimental home in Wangen a mechanic had to be sent on to the roof daily to ventilate the collectors. The air that had accumulated inside interrupted the heat flow.

Physics explains why. If water is heated in a collector during the daytime it will expand. At night it cools and contracts.

The result is suction towards the collector in the piping system, cutting off the flow of water to the pumps, as it were.

The collector sucks in air via the ventilation that is provided with the intention of letting surplus air out, and next day this air prevents water circulation.

The thrifty Swabians in Wangen were eventually fed up with fiddling about with their collectors and switched the system off. They then heated their boilers with night-rate storage heater electricity, which turned out to be less expensive.

Alfred Böbel, the project manager, costed the operation and worked out that per square metre of collector surface area the maximum power that could normally be expected in the course of a year was 500 kilowatt-hours, not the 1,600 or so that manufacturers' representatives frequently claim for them.

Assuming an active life of 10 years, each square metre of collector surface costs DM160 per annum. But 500 kilowatts of night-rate electric power cost a mere DM37.50.

His estimates for absorbers are much more encouraging. For each kilowatt-hour received by the heat pump more than three extra kilowatts can be generated. In winter 1978/79 solar heat fully heated the Wangen house for 46 days.

It did so using heat stored by the absorber and retrieved from a wet soil storage area. Since situations in which the absorbers might be expected to generate no heat at all in winter are well-nigh inconceivable over any length of time this means that the absorber can to all intents and purposes fully heat the experimental home.

© *Walter Baier* (Frankfurter Rundschau, 21 April 1980), published in English in *The German Tribune*, A Weekly Review of the German Press, 4 May 1980.

Step 24   Viewing (video counter nos. 389–421 '. . . for an unconverted house.')
Watch this section of the film with the following questions in mind, and answer them when you have the relevant information.
a)   What solar energy facilities were installed in the house in Milton Keynes ?

b)   Why is the house's thermal efficiency low ?

Step 25   Viewing (421 – the end)
The last section of film shows an unconventional house built in 1972 by an energy-conscious group called Street Farmers.

What is your group's opinion of the design of this house? (Make brief notes of the group's conclusions.)

How might the ideas this house incorporates be modified to make it acceptable to more of the general public?

NOTES

[1] *The House and the Sun*, 1974, produced by David Parham and Chris Warren, School of Architecture and Department of Fine Art, Portsmouth Polytechnic.

[2] *Towards Purity*, 1969, Institute of Water Pollution Control, University of Sheffield, Department of Civil and Structural Engineering.

11 *Copyright and the Use of Video Material*

GEOFFREY CRABB

Geoffrey Crabb is the Rights Development Officer of the Council for Educational Technology in London. He is the author of many articles and papers and provides an advisory service by way of publications and seminars. He was formerly with BBC Television, clearing rights in film material.

The current copyright legislation in Britain is contained in the Copyright Act of 1956 (referred to from now on as the Act). A perusal of it shows that such terms as *video, language laboratory*, and many others which are now in common use, do not figure at all in its wording. However, anyone using a video recorder inevitably soon stumbles into the murky world of copyright law, and in this chapter an attempt is made to provide some basic information for those working in the field of language teaching. The first part outlines the two pieces of legislation of most relevance, the second relates these to the use of video for teaching purposes and the third looks at recent and possible future developments.

1 BASIC LAW

Copyright law is the means by which the creators of certain types of material are protected from the unauthorised use of their products so that apart from being able to control its use they are in a position to negotiate fees (normally called royalties) and so derive a living. The protection takes the form of granting to the creator/producer the sole right to do or to authorise others to do certain acts in relation to the material.

In this country the Act provides protection for the following:

(a)   Literary works, being any form of words.

(b)   Dramatic and musical works.

(c)   Artistic works, including paintings, drawings, maps, charts, sculptures and photographs and all irrespective of artistic merit. Works of artistic craftsmanship, like pieces of jewellery, and works of architecture.

(d)   Sound recordings, films and broadcasts.

(e)   Published editions, being the typographical layout of a work. This item will not be referred to again as it is irrelevant in the video context.

For an individual item to be protected it need only be in material form (not just an idea in the mind), be original (not copied from something else) and must be the product of, or published by, a British subject or resident or the national of those many countries with which we have treaty obligations. No formalities have to be observed and protection is automatic from the creation of the material.

The provisions of the Act which deal with the period during which protection lasts vary from one type of material to another, but the minimum period is 50 years and in practice is almost invariably much longer and can be perpetual.

Copyright can be transferred, bought and sold just like any other property, so during the term of protection ownership may change hands many times, for example from author to publisher and from one publisher to another. To help in cases of doubt the Act states who owns copyright at the time the material is created.

Literary, dramatic, musical and artistic works
First owner is the author, composer, etc. There are a number of exceptions, the most relevant being that the first owner of the

copyright in a photograph is the person who, at the time the photograph was taken, owned the film in the camera. In addition, where a literary, dramatic or artistic work is produced by someone as part of the duties as an employee, then the employer is the first owner.

Sound recordings

First owner of the copyright is the person who, at the time the recording is made, owns the tape, disc, etc. on which the recording was made.

Films

First owner is the person paying the costs of making the film.

Broadcasts

First owner is the BBC or IBA as owners of the transmitters.

It has been said that the protection takes the form of giving to the owner of the copyright the sole right to do or authorise others to do certain acts. These are called the *restricted acts* and originally there was only one, the right to copy, which is where the term *copyright* originates. The Act, however, provides a whole series of restricted acts so the word copyright suggests a rather more restricted protection than is now the case. The range of restricted acts varies according to the type of material, but only two need concern us – namely reproducing in any material form, which is a restricted act in respect of all types of material, and giving a performance in public which applies to literary, dramatic and musical works and to sound recordings and films.

Turning briefly to the other piece of legislation of interest, these are the Performers Protection Acts. These provide that it is a criminal offence to record, film or broadcast anyone performing a work unless the recording is made for private purposes, or the inclusion of the performance is only in the background or incidental, or the written permission of the performer is first acquired. It is immaterial whether the work being performed is itself protected by copyright but it is the case that the performance must be of a 'work' – that is, something in material form. Off the cuff remarks would therefore not be protected by the Performers Protection Acts.

2   THE IMPLICATIONS FOR TEACHERS USING VIDEO

In section 1 a brief summary of two pieces of legislation has been provided, omitting much detail but giving enough information to form a basis for this section. To summarise in plain language:

(a)   Protection is given to a wide range of material including films and, it is thought, this term would extend to videotapes.

(b)   Copyright lasts for a very long term, so most items will be protected and, because of Britain's treaty obligations, this will apply to material originating from most countries. Such material will be protected to the same degree as the native product and the copyright regulations of the originating country are irrelevant.

(c)   Although the Act identifies the first owner of the copyright, ownership frequently changes hands, so tracing the owner of any particular right is sometimes difficult.

(d)   In respect of all types of material, making a copy requires the prior permission of the owner of that right. In certain cases the same applies for the right to perform in public.

(e)   It is necessary to acquire the written permission of performers before recordings or films are made unless these are for private use or the performance is only included incidentally.

It follows that permission will be required to dub or transfer onto a video tape any of the protected classes of material. Similarly, the permission of performers of works will be required before a recording may be legally made. Furthermore, to make an unauthorised copy of a videotape may infringe the copyright not only in the tape but in any copyright elements and performances on the tape. This is because the restricted act of copying applies whether the copy is made directly or indirectly, so the off-air recording of a programme may infringe not only the right in the broadcast but in those audio and videotapes being used to make the broadcast, plus any literary material (script for example) music or film material recorded on it. Before the recording may legally be made, the permission of every individual copyright owner must be acquired, together with that of any contributory performer.

Fortunately the Act does provide some relief by stating those circumstances where it is not necessary to acquire permission before copying. Unfortunately, they are of only limited value because in the 1950s when the Act was drafted, the facilities for making copies of audio and videotapes and films, either directly or off the air, were not in common use and so no special provisions were made for those wishing to do so, even for private use or for educational purposes. However, here is a summary of those most relevant.

Substantial part In respect of all types of material it is not an infringement unless the part copied is a substantial part of the whole. There are no definitions, but quality as well as quantity must be considered, so that even a small proportion of a work may be substantial if it is an important or significant part. What constitutes a substantial part of a sound recording, film or videotape is difficult to say, although in a recent case the Court of Appeal decided that the unauthorised copying of one frame of a film of *Starsky and Hutch* was an infringement.

Fair dealing for research or private study This only applies to literary, dramatic, musical and artistic works, so it is not permitted to copy sound recordings, films or videotapes even for private study, although it is permissible to copy works recorded on them. There are no definitions in the Act for 'research' 'private study' or 'fair', but it has been established that making copies for the private study of others is not permitted and 'fair' means not unduly prejudicial to the interests, and especially the commercial interests, of the copyright owner.

Educational Provisions These permit pupils and students in school to make copies of literary, dramatic, musical and artistic works in the course of instruction, provided no appliance for making multiple copies is used. This section of the Act is particularly vague and there is doubt as to whether educational establishments other than schools are covered and exactly what the term 'in the course of instruction' is intended to cover. It is clear that it is not permissible to copy sound recordings, films or videotapes because the section does not extend to these. On the other hand a video recorder is hardly likely to be regarded as a machine for making multiple copies in the same way as a photocopier obviously is, so it would be permissible to record literary, dramatic, musical and artistic works on a video recorder, provided the other conditions of the Section are observed.

Exceptions for artistic works Apart from the substantial part, fair dealing and educational provisions there are a number of ways in which artistic works may be included on film or videotape without prior permission. These are where the artistic work in question is a sculpture or work of artistic craftsmanship permanently situated in a public place or in premises open to the public; where the work is a building or other work of architecture or where any artistic work is included only incidentally or by way of background.

As for the recording or re-recording of performances, there are no exceptions to the rule that permission must be acquired, other than that relating to where the recording is made for private purposes. This would not, unfortunately, extend to recording for teaching purposes.

So, other than where an unsubstantial part is copied there are no provisions in the Acts which permit the copying of sound recordings, films or videotapes without permission, although works recorded on them may be copied subject to the limitations imposed by the fair dealing and educational provisions. Since it is impossible to record the content without also copying the carrier this is hardly helpful, but does provide some modest relief to those who are preparing their own tapes by recording existing copyright material. It is not permissible to record programmes off the air except where they are live transmissions and this is, for the ordinary viewer or listener, impossible to determine with certainty. Transmitted works may be recorded off air, subject to the limitations of fair dealing and the educational provisions.

Now a brief note on performing. To give a performance in public of literary, dramatic and musical works, sound recordings and films will require the permission of the copyright owner of all the separate elements. It is important to understand that the right to record and the right to publicly perform what has been recorded are quite separate, and the ownership of the recording and performing right may be in different hands. When acquiring permission to record it is therefore essential that if the tapes are to be used for public performance the necessary permissions are acquired at the same time. This process is made easier in respect of music and gramophone records because agencies exist which provide licences. These are, for music, The Performing Rights Society, Copyright House, Berners Street, London W1; and, for records, Phonographic Performance Ltd, 62 Oxford Street, London W1. The Act provides that where any type of material is performed in class in a school in the presence of pupils and teachers this does not constitute a public performance and permission is not required. Additionally, sound recordings may legally be played as part of the activities of an organisation devoted to educational purposes. Although this provision is of assistance where records are being played at, for example, end-of-term concerts, its value is limited because in the context of video it is unlikely that permission to dub commercial records onto video will be forthcoming, because record companies and performers are reluctant to permit this.

3 DEVELOPMENTS AND THE FUTURE OUTLOOK

Some relief has been provided by rights owners agreeing that copying and recording may be done without prior application. In other words, they have given a blanket permission to do what without it would be an infringement. Schools, adult and further education programmes listed in the *Annual Programme* of the BBC and the Independent Television Companies Association may be recorded off the air. No fee is required by the BBC but the ITCA requires a licence fee of £5 per year. Both bodies impose limits on the type of institution which may record and the period during which recordings may be retained. There are no similar arrangements for what are termed *general service programmes*

— that is, those programmes designed for general viewing. These may not be recorded even where, as in the case of *Horizon* or *Survival*, they are undoubtedly of educational value.

Similarly, there are no comprehensive schemes for the duplication of films or videotapes, but some distributors do permit copying on payment of fees. The Open University, Rank, and Guild Sound and Vision are among those which operate these arrangements.

Those producing their own video programmes may acquire permission to dub copyright music on the sound track by applying to the Mechanical Copyright Protection Society Ltd, 380 Streatham High Road, London SW16. The Society will quote a fee depending on the duration of the music to be dubbed and the extent of distribution of the programme. Regrettably, the Society cannot normally give permission to dub from commercial sound recordings, so in general users will either have to use records from mood music libraries or arrange for live performances to be recorded and then dubbed.

Before turning to possible future developments, a summary of the rather complex position outlined above may be useful. Those wishing to copy existing films or tapes may not legally do so unless:

(a)   only an unsubstantial part is being copied *or*
(b)   the film or video is being transmitted as part of the schools, further or adult education output of the BBC or ITCA and their conditions are observed *or*
(c)   permission has been acquired

Those wishing to produce their own film or tapes may not record literary, dramatic, musical or artistic works unless:

(a)   only an unsubstantial part is being copied of each protected element *or*
(b)   the recording is for the purposes of research or private study and is fair to the copyright owners *or*
(c)   the recording falls within the exemptions of the educational provisions *or*

(d)   only an artistic work is being included and the circumstances are met by the special provisions for artistic works *or*

(e)   permission has been acquired from the relevant owner of the copyright in each protected piece of material *and*

(f)   the written permission of performers has been obtained if the recording is other than for private purposes

4 RECENT AND FUTURE DEVELOPMENTS

The problems faced by the user of video material for educational purposes will illustrate the fact that the Act is out of date and no longer matches the ways in which material may be copied both in education and at home. Recognising that the legislation needed revising, a Committee of Enquiry was set up under the chairmanship of Mr Justice Whitford, and reported in March 1977. Having received a mass of evidence, much of it from educational interests, it recommended that although audio-visual recordings for private and educational purposes should be permitted, this should not be on the basis of free use but by ensuring that rights owners were properly compensated. To provide this, the Whitford Committee proposed a levy on the sale price of all equipment suitable for private recording; in other words, those items that are purchased and used in the home to copy gramophone records and record radio and television programmes. Dealing with recording for educational purposes, the Committee proposed that, in addition to paying the sales levy, an annual licence fee be paid under a negotiated blanket licensing scheme. The Committee envisaged that rights owners would combine in collecting societies and would negotiate fees and conditions with local education authorities. Both sides could then submit their views to a proposed statutory arbitration body where agreement was not forthcoming. The recommendations have found support among rights owners such as record companies and broadcasting bodies and has generally been welcomed by the educational interests. However, by the summer of 1980 the Government had still to issue a Green Paper outlining its plans for revised legislation and it is unclear as to when, or indeed if, a new copyright act will be introduced. Certainly the Committee's proposals appear to be the fairest way of reconciling the need to protect the interests of the producers of works, records, films and video material on the one hand and, on the other, the wish and need to copy and record material legally for teaching purposes. Of course the difficulties faced by educators in Britain are mirrored in other countries, and some have tried to provide relief in various ways. In Germany the sales levy already applies, but only covers making recordings for private use. Education remains unprovided for, except that there is a statutory right to record school broadcasts off the air. The new American Copyright Act of 1976 provides that 'fair use' for teaching, scholarship or research is permitted, and this appears to apply to audio visual copying and recording as much as to print copying. As with the fair dealing provisions in the Act, no definitions are included as to what is fair, although some guidance is given as to the factors that should be considered when determining if a certain use is fair. Possibly the rights owners and educational users will get together to hammer out more substantial guidelines, but in the meantime the position remains rather confused.

This chapter, in reducing the complexities of the law of copyright to its essentials, has of necessity omitted much relevant detail. It should not be taken as an authoritative day-to-day guide. Those wishing to record existing material for teaching purposes are directed to the publication *Guideline Two – Copyright Clearance – A Practical Guide*. Those engaged in the production of programmes will find *Copyright and Contract – A Course Workbook* of value. Both are available from the Council for Educational Technology, 3 Devonshire Street, London W1. The Council also issues a series of free pamphlets and booklets on copyright matters and is prepared to give advice on copyright to those who care to apply in writing.

12 *Cultural Videotapes for the ESL Classroom*

MARY ANN TELATNIK AND WILLIAM D. KRUSE

Before working at Colorado State University, Mary Ann Telatnik studied and taught at the University of California at Los Angeles. There she became very interested in the use of personal diaries to identify teacher and teaching variables and understand their effect on classroom learning.

William Kruse has been television producer and co-ordinator of television productions for the Office of Instructional Services at Colorado State University since 1965. He has produced and directed over 4000 commercial and educational television programmes.

Intensive English programmes at American universities stress the development of English proficiency in grammar, reading, writing, and listening. This is to help students pass the TOEFL or Michigan examinations as well as to meet their future academic needs. However, four to five hours of English instruction is not always effective when many students spend the remaining waking twelve to fourteen hours communicating and socialising in their native languages. This isolation fosters linguistic retardation; especially as the language of instruction is different from the language for everyday communication or for understanding the new cultural environment.

By the end of the programme the students may be ready to meet academic demands, but they are not always ready for the clashes that occur when their cultural perceptions and attitudes do not work in their new setting. In other words, their reaction to a given situation may not be the same as the expected reaction. A student from Zambia who beckoned a waitress by raising the middle finger of his right hand (an insulting, vulgar gesture in the United States) did not discover why he was thrown out of the restaurant by the manager until three months later. As problems arise due to unfamiliarity with the classroom behaviour, participation, preparation, and attitudes expected in the American university setting, cultural isolation occurs. As cultural and linguistic student groups 'ghettoize', the conflict with the community and the university intensifies. This results in the American community reacting against the foreign student community. Communication between them breaks down.

1   CULTURAL VIDEOTAPES

At Colorado State University it was decided to tackle this problem through video. Videotapes can dramatise these situations in which the foreign student encounters conflict or misunderstanding due to cultural bias or ignorance of American values and customs. The reality of television encourages conversation and the expression of attitudes and concerns. The videotapes can be played either once or many times in order for students to understand what is happening. Material for situations dramatised in the videotapes comes from the experiences of the foreign students themselves, so that the situations involve meaningful and useful information. Pragmatic situations have been emphasised: renting an apartment, cheating in the American classroom, meeting and making American friends, giving appropriate verbal and non-verbal responses in greetings and goodbyes. These situations are relatively easy to dramatise and are among the most important to help the student cope with and adjust to his American environment. The aim of the tapes is not to focus on the question of the American culture being 'right' and the foreign culture being 'wrong'; the tone and intent of the tapes are to present the American people – their values and habits – without justification, glorification, or apology. Rather, their purpose is to help the foreign student adjust to the community and university and to facilitate the attainment of his personal and educational goals. It is the student's decision either to understand and cope with his new environment or to reject it and perhaps face a difficult overseas experience. At least he is given the opportunity to explore, examine and discuss his new situation before he has to cope with his major field of studies.

The decision to develop and use videotape instruction involved a two-fold project: the actual production of the videotapes and their utilisation in the classroom.

2 PRODUCTION

Mary Ann Telatnik first tried to produce the series with a hand-held, black and white, portable video camera. In order to familiarise herself with the equipment, she practised recording people interacting both in normal, spontaneous situations and in staged situations. Problems arose: if the zoom lens wasn't used for close-ups, distance shots, or following movement, the conversation and the scene in general were stilted and boring. However, by using the zoom lens, the naturalness of conversation and behaviour was distorted or lost due to problems with focus, contrast and brightness, insufficient or too much light, and the lack of control over sound and the sound environment. All of the problematic features might be noticeable to the foreign students and therefore detract from the purpose and content of the tapes.

Now the television production facilities in the university's Office of Instructional Services are used. However, the development and production of scenarios still consume most of the time spent in developing a completed videotape lesson for the classroom. Over a period of two years, 13 scenarios have been written and recorded. (The term *scenario* is used instead of *script*, since an outline of an idea is developed and presented to volunteer 'actors'. Rather than memorise lines, the actors recreate a real-life situation of conflict or misunderstanding. In other words, the dialogue and action is improvised and spontaneous. This is easier for amateur or inexperienced actors appearing in front of a camera for the first time.)

Each scenario must clearly illustrate one idea or aspect of a problem in order to facilitate the audience's awareness and understanding. Videotapes under six minutes in length have the most dramatic effect on student discussion and participation. Therefore, the content of the scenario has to be well defined and to the point, for the sake of both the actors and the finished product.

Often a scenario is not completely defined until the actors are selected. Non-professional actors from the university community volunteer or are solicited on the basis of their experience or empathy with the main idea of the scenario. The American volunteers have usually had international experience and travel or have worked with international students. The foreign actors are indentifiable as foreigners and converse well even with accented speech which is easily understood by a foreign student audience. When the actors are given a scenario, they react to the situation in a way that is based on their own feelings and experiences. They are asked to be themselves. Changes in the situation or scenario are made on the basis of their input and suggestions. For example, when the faculty was concerned about the degree of cheating among foreign students, international students at the university were reluctant to participate in such a series. One doctoral student in electrical engineering from Egypt commented that Americans are quick to see dishonesty in foreign students, but not in themselves. Through discussions and meetings with both American and foreign students, we decided to show both an American and a foreign student caught in the act of cheating, with a factual recreation of the attitudes and actions of a university professor.

Such preliminary meetings are typical for each videotape. The actors improvise and discuss roles and feelings. They get acquainted with each other. From these sessions with the actors, the studio setting and taping procedures are established. Once in the studio, after each scene is recorded, the actors, studio personnel, the TV producer and the scenario writer criticise the tapes in relation to their believability and authenticity. Scenes are re-recorded until both qualtities are achieved.

The availability of students and faculty to act in these tapes in addition to the limitations of their class schedules has led to some interesting and productive short cuts in producing the videotapes. While exploring the difficulties of a foreign student who was having the electricity turned on in his apartment, we followed him to the utilities office, audio-taped the dialogue involved and photographed the experience on 35mm slides. This included slides of the forms needed for the transaction. This technique eliminated disruptions in the utility department and the time needed to transport the television cameras, recorders, and lights.

Figure 23

After the 35mm slides had been processed, we matched them to the previously recorded audiotape and assembled the sequence onto videotape. The student viewers followed the procedure from the audio track, and the 'frozen' action on the slides added credibility to the experience and did not detract from listening to the dialogue. Photography on 35mm slides was also used to show the same foreign student in the offices of the telephone company and the gas utility. The sales representatives then came to the television studio, where we recreated the transaction in real time and recorded it on audiotape.

Another technique was used to create a situation where a foreign student was searching the *For Rent* section on a bulletin board, presumably in a corridor on campus. The student is seen reading and rereading an advertisement and is obviously perplexed by some of the terminology. He pauses, looks toward the camera and says, 'Excuse me. Could you help me, please? I don't understand . . .' The unseen voice, complete with echo and reverberation, proceeds to answer all of his questions concerning rental jargon.

We also followed an American girl and her Iranian girlfriend around the campus and captured the adventure on 35mm slides. A dialogue between the two friends was audiotaped, edited, and matched with the slides on video for an intimate view of their relationship.

Figure 24

Another challenge was met by staging a meeting of an American girl and an Oriental girl in a classroom situation, a misunderstanding in a school corridor, and a cool reception when they meet once again in the classroom. *What really happened*? is examined by replaying the previous scenes and hearing each individual's thoughts as the action unfolds. This technique is very effective in examining this misunderstanding and creates a basis for the discussion of other potential misunderstandings (see Section 4 for script). An interesting observation of the casualness of the American culture is examined on a videotape that displays examples of different greetings and goodbyes using Latin American, Libyan, German, and American whites and blacks as they meet their respective friends at one-week, one-month, and one-year intervals.

A glossary of terms that may be encountered in a rental situation is examined visually by presenting the English word on the screen and hearing the English pronunciation and then seeing and hearing the same word translated into German, French, Chinese, Japanese, Spanish, Arabic, and Farsi.

Although these production techniques were utilised to accommodate the student and professor actors' time and availability for recording and to limit the costly on-location recordings, they do not appear to detract from the educational value of the tapes. The foreign students viewing these videotapes seem to enjoy these actualities and appear to empathise with the improvised situations. The lessons and exercises that accompany the tapes try to take advantage of this immediacy in order to enhance the learning potential of the videotapes.

3 UTILISATION

Once the tapes are recorded and edited, the second phase is to develop and co-ordinate the tapes within the curriculum of an academic ESL programme. So far, the videotapes have been used in the classroom with low, intermediate, and advanced ESL students. The Foreign Student Office has also shown the videotapes during orientation programmes for international students entering Colorado State University with a minimum 550 TOEFL score. With these students and advanced ESL students the discussion generated by these tapes is supplemented with problem-solving activities. These exercises help to develop not only students' vocabulary and communication, but also an awareness of themselves in their new environment. For example, along with the videotape on friendship, one exercise is to rank fifteen adjectives from the most to the least typical when describing Americans. The students are given the opportunity to express their opinions and discuss their experiences with others. They must also come to a consensus-ranking of the adjectives as a group. This process prepares them for the work necessary in many graduate seminars in American universities where they must arrive at a consensus and defend their reasons or opinions.

With low and intermediate-level students, several varieties of worksheets and exercises help to increase vocabulary and improve listening and grammar skills. Because the language on the tape is natural, American actors especially use more slang and informal expressions. The student has the opportunity to increase his passive if not his active vocabulary of two-word verbs. He can also make comparisons between formal and informal language. Grammar and syntax concepts can also be illustrated via the videotapes, and practised. With the videotapes on cheating, signing an apartment lease, or friendship, the present and past uses of modals are easily demonstrated. Contextualised lessons based on information in the videotapes can either review or drill a structure presented in grammar or writing classes.

Current events can be integrated into the lessons. Articles or programmes from community or campus newspapers or radio/TV programmes can be outside reading or listening assignments. In class, the students can compare and/or contrast the information with that of the videotapes. Articles can be used as cloze passages to reinforce grammar, writing, or vocabulary lessons. Once completed, they can be discussed in terms of the content of the lesson.

Because the emphasis is on participation and skill development in communication and awareness, testing has not been developed with the videotapes. We are not interested so much in testing the students' understanding and/or ability to reconstruct the content of the videotapes as in their being able to discuss and understand the intent of the videotapes. The worksheets on vocabulary, problem-solving, and grammar give the student the physical 'proof' of their having learned something, while the experience of asking and answering questions and defending and clarifying their ideas and opinions hopefully gives them the confidence and skill to communicate in social and academic situations. The use of the videotapes maintains a uniform core of instruction for the student to test himself in terms of his second language development and his cultural awareness.

Figure 25   *William Kruse and Mary Anne Telatnik discussing Friendliness vs. Friendship*

4   FRIENDLINESS vs. FRIENDSHIP

SCENE 1:   Classroom

Professor: Now as you know, chapter 1 should be read carefully. I have been known at times in my career to give a quiz the first thing right out after the first meeting. Therefore, I would urge you to read chapter 1 carefully. I guess that's all. We'll see you next Wednesday at 11 o'clock. Have a good day.

Susan: Looks like it's going to be a really rough semester, doesn't it?

Beniko:	Yes, it does.
Susan:	Are you new here?
Beniko:	Yes, I am.
Susan:	What's your name?
Beniko:	Beniko. What's yours?
Susan:	Susan. What are you studying here?
Beniko:	I am planning to get a Master's degree in TEFL.
Susan:	That's Teaching English as a Foreign Language. Are you planning to go back to Japan to teach?
Beniko:	Yes, I hope so.
Susan:	Are you taking any of the Linguistic classes?
Beniko:	I'll be taking E 520, E 526, and E507.
Susan:	We're going to have some of the same classes besides this one. Well, it's almost noon. Do you want to go over to the Student Centre and get some coffee or something to eat?
Beniko:	Yes, sure.
Susan:	Okay. Let's go.

SCENE 3:	In class later
Susan:	Hi.
Beniko:	Hello.
Susan:	How are you?
Beniko:	Fine.
Susan:	Did you get the assignment read?

SCENE 2:	The following Wednesday
Boyfriend:	Why don't we go out for a little dinner and a drive and maybe a movie.
Susan:	Sounds good. Can we talk about this later?
Boyfriend:	What's the rush?
Susan:	I've got to get to the bookstore before class.
Boyfriend:	I'll pick you up at 8.
Susan:	Beniko, I'll talk to you later. I've got to rush.
Beniko:	Hmmm.
Susan:	Did you understand everything?

Professor: I think it's time to begin. I presume that all of you got your textbooks from the student store and I do hope that you got a chance to read chapter 1. That really sets the scene. It begins to show you a little bit of what history is all about from the eyes and the ears and the feelings of those ancient Greek peoples.

Commentary: Now let's look at what really happened.

SCENE 1: (Replay – Beniko and Susan's thoughts are recorded over the action).

Susan: What a cute girl. I'd really like to get to know her.

Beniko: She seems really nice. I really need a good girlfriend to talk to. I hope we can get along well.

SCENE 2: (Replay)

Susan: I'm glad I saw Beniko. But I can't really stop and talk to her right now. Oh well, I can always talk to her in class.

Beniko: I thought she was nice. She could have a moment to talk to me. How rude of her to run away from me like this. She was too nice to me at first; she doesn't like me because I am a foreigner. I feel that I am mistreated.

SCENE 3:

Beniko: Gee, what does she want now? She talks to me when she wants to and ignores me when she doesn't have time. She's not going to treat me as a fully-fledged person because I'm a foreigner anyway.

Susan: What in the world is going on! These foreigners sure are a moody bunch. Well, I don't know what else I can do now.

The following questions appear one at a time on the screen:
How do you feel about this relationship?

What *is* the difference between 'friend' and 'friendly'? and between 'friendliness' and 'friendship'?

13 BOCS: A Multi-Media General English Course

GILLIAN JONES

Gillian Jones taught EFL in Spain, Portugal and Colombia before going to the British Council Teaching Centre in Teheran. There she worked on a materials-writing project as well as in teacher training. At present she works freelance and is based in Germany.

1 GENERAL BACKGROUND

In 1976 the British Council in Iran had decided to give greater priority to its own teaching of English in its ELT policy, and began a process of curriculum innovation in its six teaching centres. The aim was to provide exemplary models of programme design and methodology in both EMG programmes (English for Mixed Groups of learners) and its ESG programme (English for Special Groups of learners). The design and implementation of EMG programmes was centralised in the Tehran centre and a first concern was to develop a house style that would be common to all six centres – Isfahan, Shiraz, Mashed, Tabriz, Ahwaz and Tehran. Because of the geographical separation of the six centres and the need for provincial centres to see what was going on at the Tehran centre and to comment creatively on its proposals, much use was made of video in staff training sessions.

2 THE BOCS PROJECT

Curriculum innovation cannot be imposed on teaching staff, and accordingly staff training was used as a means to involve teaching staff in the process of curriculum redesign. The first set of staff training programmes consisted of a mix of video and printed material. Below is an extract from an overview paper which was circulated amongst staff.

DESIGNING A PROGRAMME

The problem   To design and develop a 60-hour programme to be called Basic Oral Communication Skills in English (BOCS) for adult remedial beginners.

Constraints   BOCS has to cater for a level of entry characterised by:

(1) A defective grammar that generates confused syntax ('I am having a bad headache').

(2) An inherited learning style that sees language as an object of knowledge rather than an instrument of communication ('a lesson is a list of items to be learned').

(3) A previous teaching pattern that has focused on grammatical accuracy and largely excluded conversational practice ('the teacher gives the grammar: it's up to the student, somehow, to use it').

(4) A wish to converse as a status accomplishment ('English is a good thing and I want it').

(5) A wish for magical methods, instant payoff ('I want it now').

Resources   BOCS can call on experience in using an adapted version of *Say What you Mean in English* by J. Andrews (Nelson) and the media resources that have been used with it (OHPs, lab drills, video programme, etc.)

Intention   To use BOCS

(1) as a means of converting the usual hesitant product of the secondary system into a more self-propelled and confident user of English who is capable, on satisfactory completion of BOCS, of undertaking a three-year 360-hour programme leading to the Cambridge FCE examination.

(2) as a three-week intensive threshold programme in English for Study Travel Abroad projects for special groups before they go on to more technical English.

Background papers were prepared and circulated. The main issues were discussed in a partially scripted video presentation featuring senior ELT staff in Tehran. Group discussion then followed. Feedback on the form and content of the programmes was summarised by a group secretary − a different member from each centre for each programme. This was how the BOCS project was born.

EMG programmes were designed in 60-hour stages, of which BOCS was to be the first. The aim was to bring students to the point where they could enter a final 60-hour course of preparation for the First Certificate in English examination after some 360 hours. Courses were originally planned around existing commercially produced materials and the earlier programmes were characterised by a rich audio-visual mix. Each classroom was given OHP, audio cassette and video playback facilities, though video systems had to be shared and at peak hours were not available to all classes simultaneously.

3   THE STUDENTS

A typical EMG One student had studied six years of English in high school. He or she had learnt a lot of grammatical rules by heart in Persian and lists of English vocabulary. The ability to use this knowledge in oral communication was small. Nevertheless, to appear to be going back to square one would be extremely discouraging to students, and for BOCS a new approach was needed. It had to be an approach which made use of the English that students already had at their command.

4   BOCS DESIGN

Initially the BOCS syllabus was seen as requiring a double approach. On the one hand notional−functional categories such as greetings and enquiries, suggesting and requesting action, etc., were seen as an appropriate type of objective for the course to aim at. On the other hand, it was recognised that a rhetorical syllabus based on conversational strategies was essential. This meant that the essential unit of learning was not to be the *sentence*, but rather the *moves* a speaker would make in pursuit of some objective in conversational exchange. Learners were to be encouraged to initiate and respond to conversational moves — so that they would be aware of strategies for requesting something and responding positively and negatively to a request — and to vary their strategies according to social circumstances. The aim of a BOCS lesson was thus to develop conscious strategies for interacting in a specific type of exchange. The role for video was to present models of such exchanges. These models would provide a target in terms of language performance, for students to aim at. In this way the aims of the course were made explicit at every stage. Students were also conscious of the development of conversational strategies and this was achieved to a large extent by the metalinguistic labelling of moves. At a later stage, video would again be used to revise and provide a stimulus for role-play.

5 METHODOLOGY

The emphasis in classroom procedure is on activity, and the culminating point and test of students' achievement in a unit is the role-play stage. The earlier stages of a unit, for psychological as well as pedagogical reasons, employ quite traditional teaching methods. Wall pictures (on OHP transparency) and recorded dialogues are plentiful and help, by creating the necessary contexts, to take the student into situations in the world outside the classroom.

6 USING COMMERCIALLY PRODUCED VIDEO MATERIAL

Producing video material is time consuming and expensive, and it was decided that the video component of BOCS should not be produced until the course had been piloted with classes at least once. Thus for the first year, BOCS classes used video material that was commercially available: *On We Go* (BBC English by Television). This the students found both useful and enjoyable to work with. The series used was however more appropriate to a structural than a functional course. It consisted of 15-minute sequences, each one containing a story-line and featuring a particular group of characters, punctuated at intervals by two or three minutes of structure drilling which the students joined in. The style of presentation was somewhat dated and culturally the series was very clearly situated in England. This was inappropriate. Few of the BOCS students were actually planning to visit England; most needed their English for use in Iran and to communicate with a variety of other nationalities in their work. It was evident that video material suitable for the new course was not available commercially and would have to be produced in the centre if it was to be an integral part of the course. In fact, at the same time that video had been installed in the classrooms, the Tehran centre had been equipped with a recording studio, booth and editing facilities.

7   VIDEO COMPONENT

The BOCS video component was planned as a series of short − three to four minute − sequences. They would feature the sort of people in encounters and situations relevant to the students' needs. The aim of each sequence was to present an example of the particular kind of exchange which was the aim of that unit of the course. It would introduce some but not all of the language items in the unit. The captions preceding each unit named the functions dealt with. The second aim of the sequences was to act as a stimulus and a jumping off point for role play. Teachers' notes would suggest ways in which the teacher could guide students from a fairly imitative performance of what they had seen on the screen to original and creative role-play in parallel situations.

8 MAKING THE VIDEO SEQUENCES

As room space was a valuable commodity in the Tehran teaching centre the recording studio, when not in use as such, opened out into an examinations and general purpose hall. This was not an ideal arrangement. Nevertheless it provides a good example of how a recording studio can be made available without totally monopolising valuable space. To improve the sound, the walls were hung with curtains of heavy material. The studio was equipped with portable lighting equipment, a studio camera (a second was acquired later) and a portapak camera (which could be used in the studio as well as outside on location) and microphones. Off the studio was the recording booth, equipped with monitors and facilities for vision mixing. The producer in the booth had sound contact with the camera operators in the studio, although she was not able to see them. A team of three people operated the equipment. The educational technologist who headed the team had a background of EFL. In consultation with the writers of the BOCS materials, she wrote the scripts and directed and produced the series. Assisting her were an engineer responsible for technical direction and a technical assistant. The actors were all teachers or other members of the centre's staff, and in fact the teachers soon became quite skilled as camera operators and were able to help in this way too. Besides the scripting, rehearsing and the actual recording of the sequences there was also the meticulous job of editing and the final process of duplicating copies so that all the centres should have enough. The team available was the minimum number needed to cope with these various aspects of the project and they were able to call upon the services of a graphics artist who designed the captions.

LESSONS LEARNT

The BOCS video sequences Series I were produced and recorded towards the end of the first year of the BOCS project. All the units of the course had by this time been piloted with a limited number of·

classes in Tehran and three regional centres. Recording took place either in the studio or in locations where the portapak camera could be used. Locations included the British Council garden, a nearby tennis court, the library and the teaching centre coffee bar. The main lesson learnt from the location sequences was the need to and difficulty of controlling extraneous noise. Small unwanted noises such as the clinking of crockery in the coffee bar proved to be distracting in the actual sequence – although good arguments could be made for leaving them in. Much greater interference came from the noise of traffic in nearby streets. This was impossible to exclude and was the reason why outside locations were abandoned in the revised series.

A second and vital lesson was learnt from the production of Series I. This was the need to consider the process of editing at the time of the actual recording. Failure to do so sufficiently made the job of editing Series I extremely difficult and had considerable effect on the finished product. The problem arose because camera shots were too 'tight' at the beginning and end of each shot at the points where they had to be edited together. A few seconds of recording are inevitably lost in the process of editing shots together. If the camera man does not allow for this, he makes the editor's job extremely difficult. If a shot starts with the actual words and picture which are required in the finished version the job is virtually impossible and a part of it is bound to be clipped off and lost. Even if the editor were skilled enough not to lose any of the dialogue, such tight editing meant that the final effect was highly concentrated and very demanding of the student both visually and in terms of listening.

The revised series benefited from the experience of Series I in this respect. Visually the pace is slower, allowing students more time to process the information on the screen. This is achieved by allowing the camera to take longer on its shots. Linguistically, too, the pace is slower. The pace of speech is not slowed down artificially but natural pauses are provided to break up the flow of speech, as happens normally. For example, a character pauses in mid-sentence to light a cigarette or pull up a chair. Such pauses were written into the script in the revised version. They were helpful also from the teacher's point of view, providing points to 'pause' the tape in order to ask or answer questions or to draw students' attention to details of language.

The BOCS video sequences, as indicated, were made twice. The first time was towards the end of the first year of the project, and the second a year later in summer 1978 when the course had undergone revision and been printed on the centre's offset litho. The revised series consists of twelve sequences divided into three blocks. Three lengthier revision units occur between units 5 and 6, units 9 and 10 and after unit 12. The three blocks each follow a story-line that adds an element of surprise and interest. The following notes refer to the revised version. Outside locations have been abandoned and sound quality is greatly improved. The pacing is better and the lessons learnt from editing Series I result in a more relaxed sequence of camera shots.

In unit 10 a new library assistant is introduced to the librarian at the British Council library. The new assistant subsequently turns out to be far from ideal for the job. In this unit of BOCS the focus is on asking for permission.

UNIT 10

Setting: Library
Characters: Sally Gilbert (librarian), Patrick Villa (senior librarian), Ann Wilson, Customer.

Dialogue	*Functions*
PV enters with Ann Wilson	
PV: Good morning Sally.	
S: Oh, good morning Mr Villa.	
PV: Can I introduce Miss Wilson? She's our new library assistant.	
S: Hullo. Nice to meet you.	
A: Hullo.	
PV: Will you tell Miss Wilson about the library, please? I have to go to a meeting.	*Request action* *Obligation*

S:	Yes of course. Come round here. Let's start with the library cards.	*Suggestion*

fade

S:	Do you understand that?	
A:	Oh yes.	
S:	Right. Now let's look at . . .	
A:	Is it all right if I smoke?	*Request permission*
S:	No I'm afraid not.	*Objection*
	'No Smoking' sign	
	Not in here.	
A:	Well, why don't we go and have a coffee.	*Suggestion*
S:	No I'd rather not. I'm very busy.	*Objection Reason*
A:	Well do you mind if I go?	*Request permission*
S:	Well all right. But don't be long. The library opens in ten minutes.	*Warning*

fade

S:	Can you help, please, Miss Wilson?	*Request action*
Customer:	Oh excuse me.	
A:	Yes?	
Customer:	I want to take out these six books. Is it all right?	*Request permission*
A:	Yes sure. Go ahead.	
S:	Oh no, I'm sorry. You can only take 3 books.	*Objection*
	Look. You'd better read the rules first.	*Advice*

A: Oh OK. But do you mind if I   *Request permission*
            make a phone call first?
S: Well all right. But be quick.
            We're very busy.

9   TEACHING FROM THE VIDEO SEQUENCES

The Teacher's Guide gives detailed suggestions as to how to exploit
each video sequence. In general, however, the original intention
was that the sequences should provide a learning target, by framing
the type of exchange which is the aim of each unit. With this in
mind the suggested procedure is to show the sequence at the
beginning of each unit. A certain amount of redundant language is
scripted into each sequence, and the task for students at first can
seem a daunting one. The aim however is to help them to recognise
redundancy and to encourage them to go for the gist of an
exchange – by identifying moves rather than attempting to
identify every word. The purpose of the first viewing is for students
to identify language functions. The Teacher's Guide suggests
appropriate questions and indicates where to stop and ask them.
The class returns to the video sequence after working through the
main body of the material provided by the course book. This would
be towards the end of the unit and as a preparation for role-play.
The work at this stage is more detailed and intensive with students
acting out what they see on the screen. Parallel or related situations
are then the subject of student role-play.

  Not all teachers followed this suggested procedure. For some,
such a brief initial viewing was disconcerting and they preferred to
reserve the video sequence for later in the unit and then exploit it
much as one would a listening comprehension passage. The video
sequences and the course book material feature two different sets
of characters and some teachers preferred to keep the two separate.
The Teacher's Guide for the revised series adopts a flexible
approach on this question. The extract in below from the *Teacher's
Guide* to unit 4 proposes a point near the beginning of the unit for a
focus question, suggests a viewing procedure and gives ideas for

role-play. The video sequence shows Judy buying tickets for a concert recital at the British Council.

Suggested treatment

1 Play opening sequence: close-up of concert poster; Judy goes to desk.

Establish all information students have got from poster: Recital. Date. Seat prices.

Focus question: What does Judy want?

2 Play whole sequence from the beginning.

3 Establish answers to focus question. How many tickets? Which day? What price?

4 For second replay ask students to put up their hands when there is a *request clarification* or *request repetition.*

Replay and stop as these points are reached.

Why does Judy not understand the price?

5 Replay whole sequence.

6 The poster idea could be used for role-play prompts — put several on board, different types of concert, dates, prices, to give prompts for *request directions*, other alternatives, etc.
